LONE WOLF 2100

PATTERN STORM

Inspired by the classic manga
series **Lone Wolf and Cub** by
KAZUO KOIKE
and
GOSEKI KOJIMA

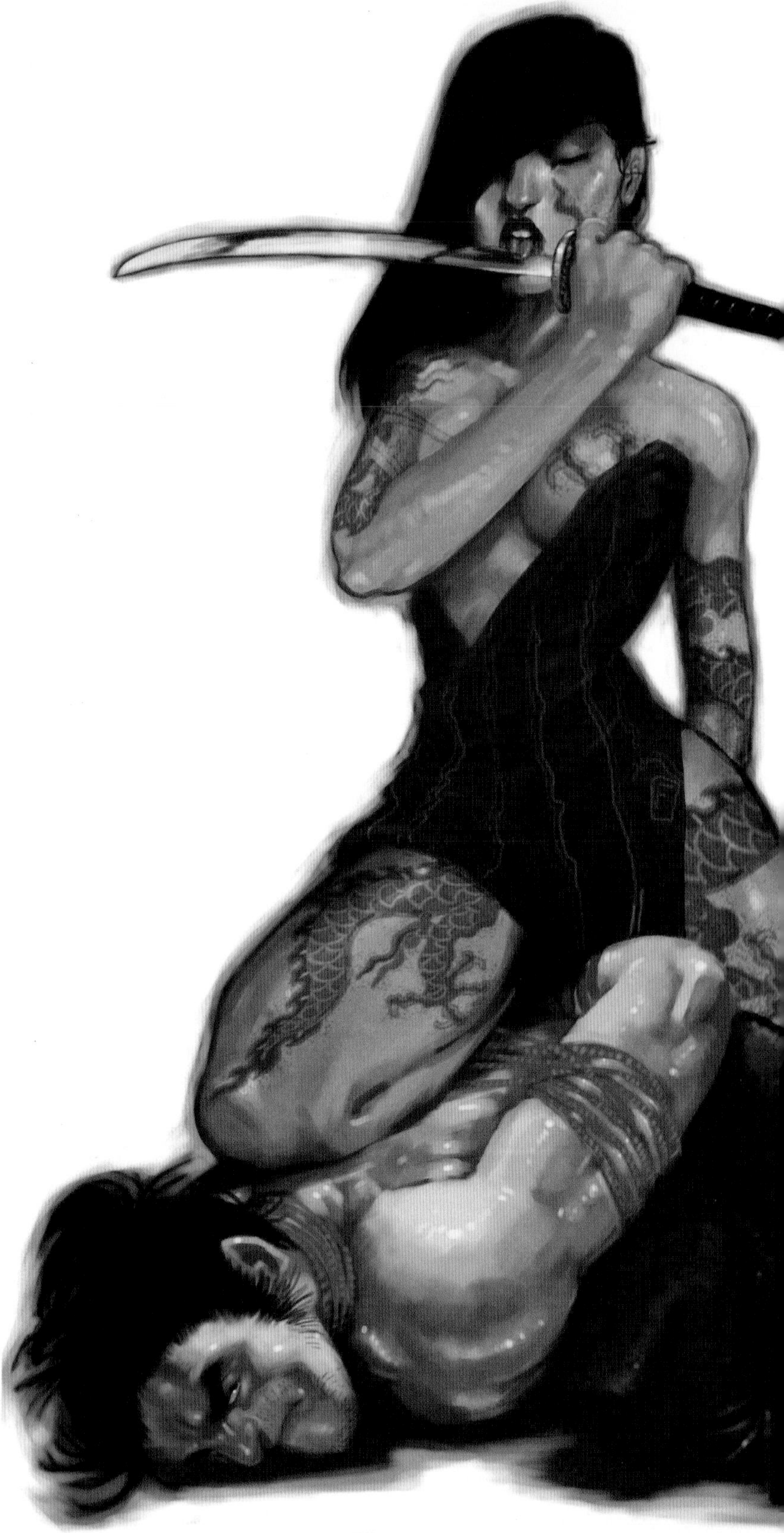

LONE WOLF 2100 ™

子連水狼

PATTERN STORM

written by
MIKE KENNEDY

art by
FRANCISCO RUIZ VELASCO

lettering by
SNO CONE STUDIOS

™
Dark Horse Books™

publisher
MIKE RICHARDSON

collection designer
DARIN FABRICK

art director
LIA RIBACCHI

assistant editor
JEREMY BARLOW

editor
RANDY STRADLEY

LONE WOLF 2100 Volume 3 — PATTERN STORM
Lone Wolf 2100™ copyright © 2004 Dark Horse Comics, Inc. and
Koike Shoin. Dark Horse Books™, Dark Horse Comics®, and the
Dark Horse logo are trademarks of Dark Horse Comics, Inc.,
registered in various categories and countries. All rights reserved.
No portion of this publication may be reproduced or transmitted,
in any form or by any means, without the express written
permission of Dark Horse Comics, Inc. Names, characters, places,
and incidents featured in this publication either are the product
of the author's imagination or are used fictitiously. Any
resemblance to actual persons (living or dead), events, institutions,
or locales, without satiric intent, is coincidental.

This volume collects issues nine through eleven
of the comic-book series, **Lone Wolf 2100**,
plus the one-shot **"The Red File."**

Published by Dark Horse Books
A division of Dark Horse Comics, Inc.
10956 SE Main Street
Milwaukie, OR 97222

www.darkhorse.com

Comic Shop Locator Service (toll-free):
1-888-266-4226

First edition:
ISBN: 1-59307- 079-9

1 3 5 7 9 10 8 6 4 2
Printed in China

UNITED NATIONS/ CORPORATIONS INVESTIGATIVE ARM

TOP SECRET EYES ONLY

The following materials were retrieved under the guise of a Pan-National Congressional Audit. Access was allowed as per international law, and all personal communication was secured and restored from permanent archive. No data was lost or destroyed in the course of events, except as noted.

Files classified as RED were accessible only to those of Executive Clearance, including the A.S.E. (Avatar to the Supreme Executive) d. Terasawa, and those granted clearance by qualified individuals. By definition, files classified as RED were either hard materials to be destroyed or digital correspondence printed once, then stricken from digital storage. These files, however, remained physically intact inside a secure lockbox within the A.S.E.'s private quarters for reasons unknown. As this residence was issued by Cygnat Owari Corporate Housing, access was granted during Congressional Subpoena.

Further investigation has continued since acquiring these files, yet no additional insight as to why they remained undestroyed has been discovered.

CYG
PRIM
EXECU

ecutive Cleara
S.E. (Avatar
xecutive) d
granted cle
individua
classifie
mater
corr
st

priva
As this residenc
Owari Corporate Housing
was granted.

TOP SE
EYES ONLY

子連れ狼

2100

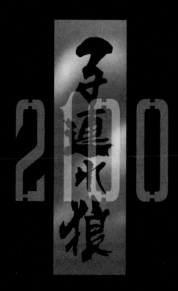

PRESSNET

History of Sungshan, Taiwan.

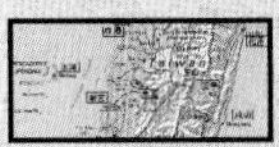

Timeline of events leading to the firebombing.

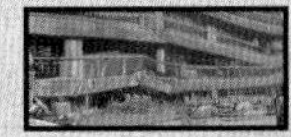

Registry of known victims.

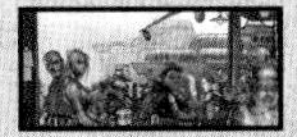

Public poll: Do you agree?

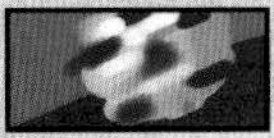

- World Cup: Mexico wins again!

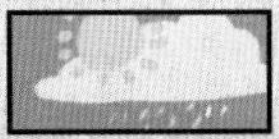

Local forecast

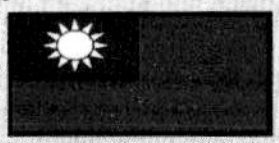

Regional news

ARCHIVES

TAIWANESE CITY DESTROYED

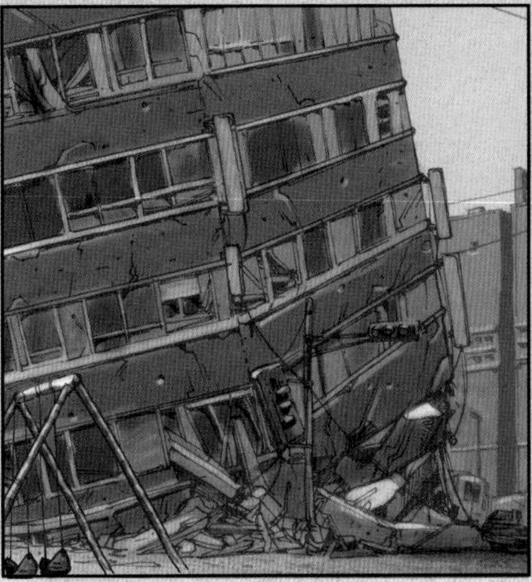

Globalnet Newswire, Taiwan (GNN) – "Sungshan is no more." Those were the opening words in World Health Secretary Brandon Major-Smith's press conference held yesterday in Hong Kong's Re-Colonized Capital building. Major-smith confirmed rumors that the industrial center of Taiwan had indeed been secured by military forces in an attempt to contain a deadly virus that had spread through the population in less than 3 days. According to Major-Smith, a collection of the world's most prolific scientists were consulted, and it was largely agreed that the only chance of containing the organism was through regional fire-bombing.

"We are confident the danger has passed, and that the sterilization of the area was successful. Our compassion goes out to the families of those victims trapped in the hot zone."

The World Health Consortium has taken severe criticism from human right activists and governments worldwide who believe their absolute condemnation of an entire region's population was akin to genocide. Major-Smith begs to differ.

"Those unfortunates caught within the secured region of Sungshan would have died within 48 hours from this plague anyway, and such death would not have contributed to a solution. As inhumane as these groups might believe our action to be, it was the only way to prevent an even greater disaster. Had this action not been taken, it is possible the entire island of Taiwan would now be infected, with international shipping lanes threatening to spread the disease worldwide. We did the only thing that could be done."

The plague responsible for this disaster is believed to be the product of manmade genetic engineering, and has been labeled "The War Spore" by various radical organizations. Though no single group or individual has been linked to its release, widespread belief holds The Coalition for Universal Life responsible. The Coalition has openly claimed responsibility for the bombing of several EmCon factories in the past several months, and reports of recent activity around Sungshan, an industrial center in the manufacture of EmCon components, have been openly verified by Coalition spokesmembers. The group denies responsibility for the War Spore's release, however.

"While we regret the loss of human life in this tragedy, we cannot share any grief in the government-sanctioned destruction of the slave-trading corporate structures housed in Sungshan," says Coalition spokesperson Valerie Proust. "Perhaps now our Emulated brethren will be valued more as genetic beings deserving equal rights instead of exploitable machinery whose parts are now merely harder to come by."

"These are not unlike issues dealt with 60 years ago, when cloning became commonplace," says Major-Smith. (*more*)

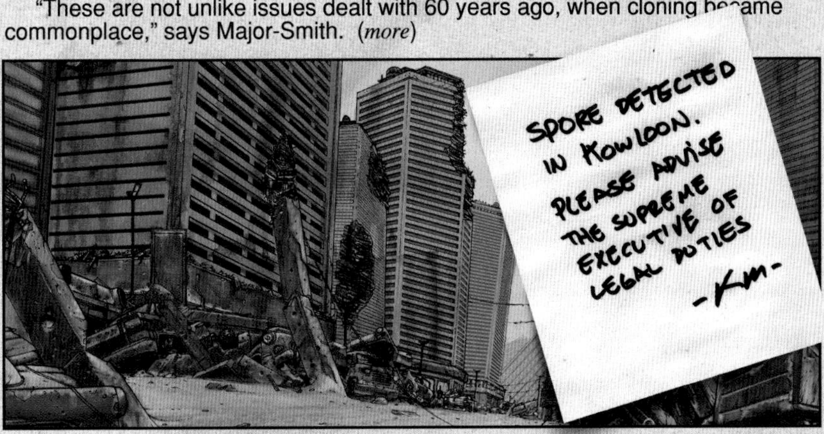
SPORE DETECTED IN KOWLOON.
PLEASE ADVISE THE SUPREME EXECUTIVE OF LEGAL DUTIES
-Kim-

CYGNAT OWARI
Primary Research Campus
Executive Legal Consultation and Policy

General Internal Memorandum:

To all employees:

In light of recent environmental conditions, Cygnat Owari has been solicited by The World Health Consortium for a number of departmental audits. These audits should be scheduled and routed through Legal Consultation only. DO NOT SPEAK OF ANY INTERNAL MATTERS WITH OUTSIDE PARTIES WITHOUT CONSULTING WITH LEGAL FIRST. This includes even the most innocuous third party – friends, spouses, relatives, etc. Should it be discovered that any information has left the compound without authorization, you could be held liable to the full extent of prosecution.

In response to the heightened tension surrounding these legal matters, we are increasing security around the campus to include a number of military class automatons. Their presence is to insure your safety.

With everyone's cooperation and dedication, we will see these questionable times through successfully. Your loyalty and support is the bedrock on which Cygnat Owari stands — without your strength and talent, we are nothing.

Thank you,

Kristiana Martinez
Senior Executive Legal Consultant"

51995>

9 781569 717578

USER-AGENT: Delphonia-Userlink / MSP InternalPassport / AuxTalkEncoded
FROM: Bunkasa Ishima, RDev #603092
TO: Designation ID - "Terasawa", SupEx Attachment #292093
DATE: Thursday, June 18th, 2099 10:38:28
SUBJECT: Re: Task Units

As requested, please find the attached information on Task Units Bravo 14-17.

Each has been tested in secluded field exams and subjected to stress conditions several degrees beyond standard. The results, as outlined within, were quite satisfactory.

The host components have been cleared through quarantine, and no sign of biological-rejection has been detected. These units can be given final tracking implants for free-roaming exercises and made available within 3 days. Please advise.

Note: Though these units were designed for the Supreme Executive himself, based on his exact specifications, I am confident we can achieve more efficient field units with similar capabilities through an extension of our standard Emulation Construct program. If prudent, I would be happy to outline a proposal for the Executive Committee. Please advise.

- B.Ishikawa

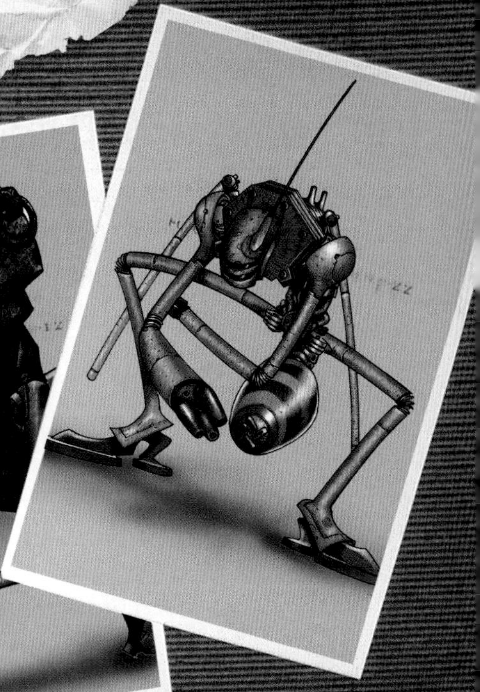

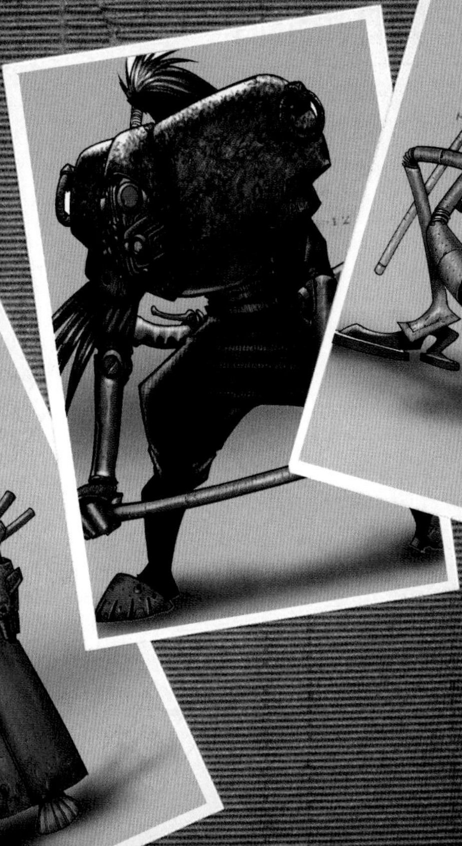

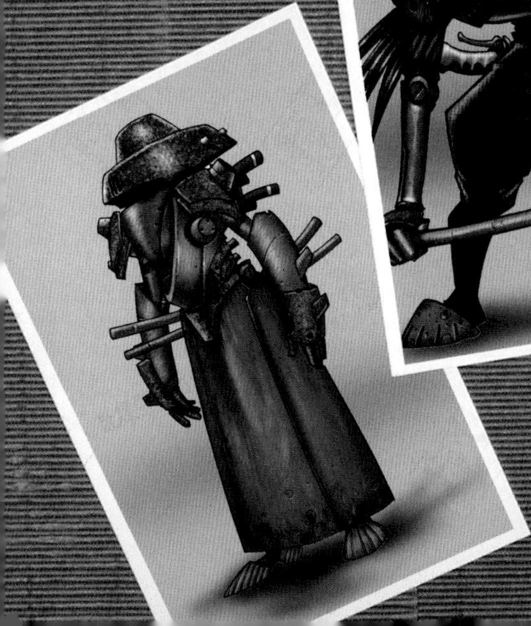

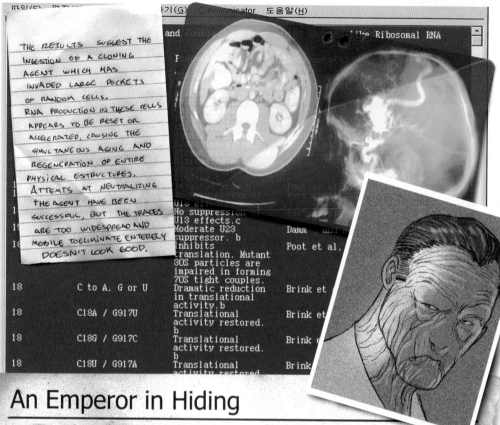

and ... Ribosomal RNA

THE RESULTS SUGGEST THE
INGESTION OF A CLONING
AGENT WHICH HAS
INVADED LARGE POCKETS
OF RANDOM CELLS.
RNA PRODUCTION IN THESE CELLS
APPEARS TO BE RESET OR
ACCELERATED, CAUSING THE
SIMULTANEOUS AGING AND
REGENERATION OF ENTIRE
PHYSICAL ESTRUCTURES.
ATTEMPTS AT NEUTRALIZING
THE AGENT HAVE BEEN
SUCCESSFUL, BUT THE TRACES
ARE TOO WIDESPREAD AND
MOBILE TOELIMINATE ENTERELY
DOESN'T LOOK GOOD.

		No suppression	
		U13 effects.c	
		Moderate U23 suppressor. b	Damon ...
		Inhibits translation. Mutant 30S particles are impaired in forming 70S tight couples.	Poot et al.
18	C to A, G or U	Dramatic reduction in translational activity.b	Brink et ...
18	C18A / G917U	Translational activity restored. b	Brink et ...
18	C18G / G917C	Translational activity restored. b	Brink e...
18	C18U / G917A	Translational activity restored.	Brink...

An Emperor in Hiding

16 July 2099 — It has been nearly three months since Lucca Bialissimo, Supreme Executive of leading bio-synthetic development conglomerate Cygnat Owari, has been seen by the public. Though the international influence of his company continues to thrive with little competition to speak of, the once-flamboyant centerpiece of Cygnat Owari PR has become noticeably absent from the public eye. His office no longer returns phone calls. His press secretary no longer schedules trips around the world. Even his private mansion in Malaysia seems to grow stagnant and unkempt, leading many to wonder whether foul play is involved.

Such concerns were put to rest, however, when Bialissimo's EmCon Avatar designated Terasawa announced to the world that his employer was suffering from health problems, and had taken to self-imposed exile until the debilitating condition could be corrected. Details of the illness were not made available, but it is believed to include certain disfiguring symptoms, symptoms that Bialissimo feels are too humbling to be seen or photographed by the public.

For decades, Bialissimo was known as the sharpest corporate playboy on the planet, hosting parties and events that not only drew great spectacle, but often perpetuated his enormous fortune through clever negotiation of broadcast rights and likeness royalties. He has been romantically linked with

CYGNAT OWARI

On behalf of our absent leader, it is my great honor to lead you as his personal Avatar. Make no mistake, his heart and mind are focused on the continued success of Cygnat Owari and the satisfaction of its employees.

These are dark times, and as we continue to face legal concerns following the tragic release of The War Spore, we will dedicate ourselves to curing that very plague threatening mankind. Cygnat Owari boasts the most talented and gifted bio-chemists the world has ever known, and we are confident there is no situation or virus that cannot be disassembled.

In order to insure the safety of our employees, security will be tightened and redefined under the watchful eye of a new Inner Security Team, lead by designated_Belladonna. These Inner Security Units will be assigned to specific individuals and departments, and will provide the same degree of protection as the much less subtle Ara Units.

Details of this program will be distributed at group meetings currently being scheduled.

Thank you, and let us continue on towards greatness.

d.Terasawa
...fice of The Supreme

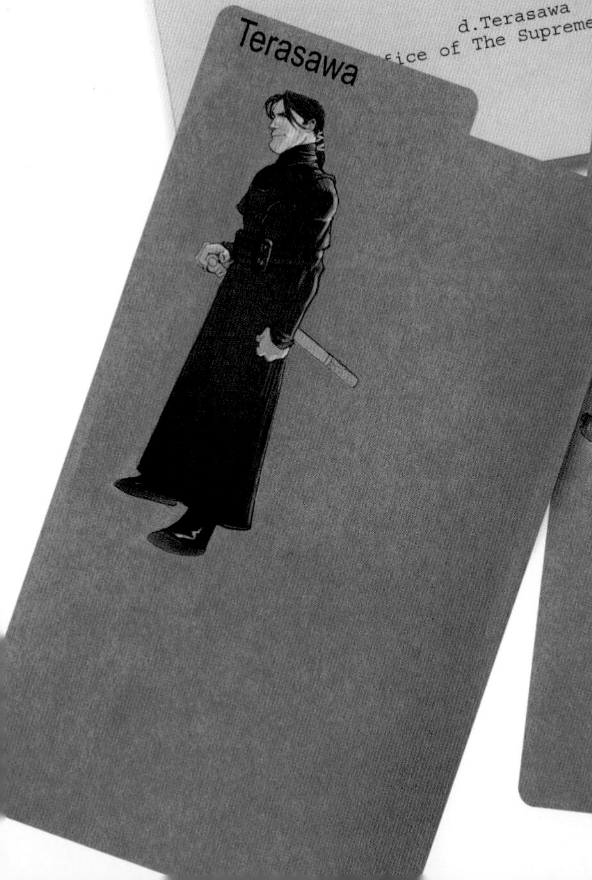
Terasawa

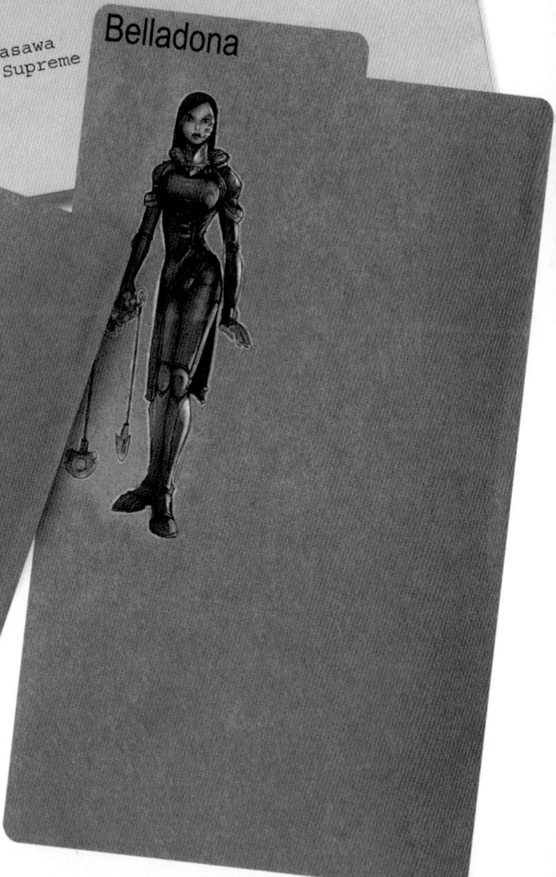
Belladona

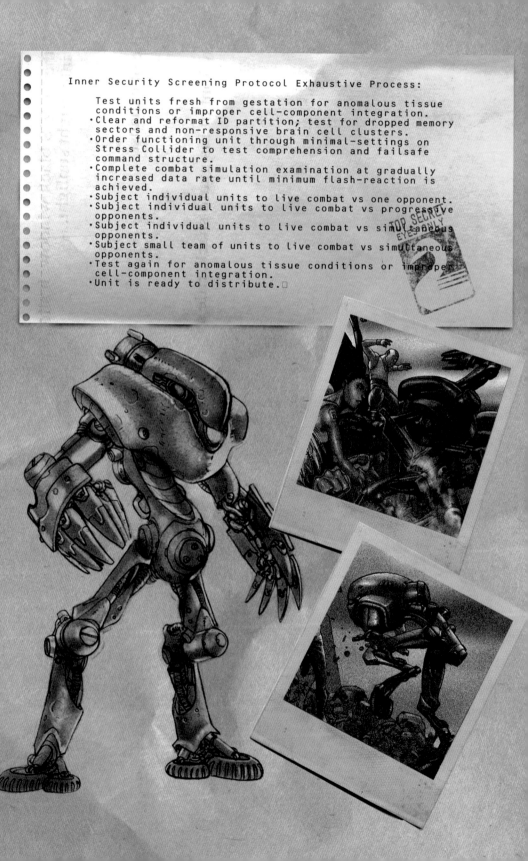

Inner Security Screening Protocol Exhaustive Process:

Test units fresh from gestation for anomalous tissue conditions or improper cell-component integration.

- Clear and reformat ID partition; test for dropped memory sectors and non-responsive brain cell clusters.
- Order functioning unit through minimal-settings on Stress Collider to test comprehension and failsafe command structure.
- Complete combat simulation examination at gradually increased data rate until minimum flash-reaction is achieved.
- Subject individual units to live combat vs one opponent.
- Subject individual units to live combat vs progressive opponents.
- Subject individual units to live combat vs simultaneous opponents.
- Subject small team of units to live combat vs simultaneous opponents.
- Test again for anomalous tissue conditions or improper cell-component integration.
- Unit is ready to distribute.

TOP SECRET
EYES ONLY

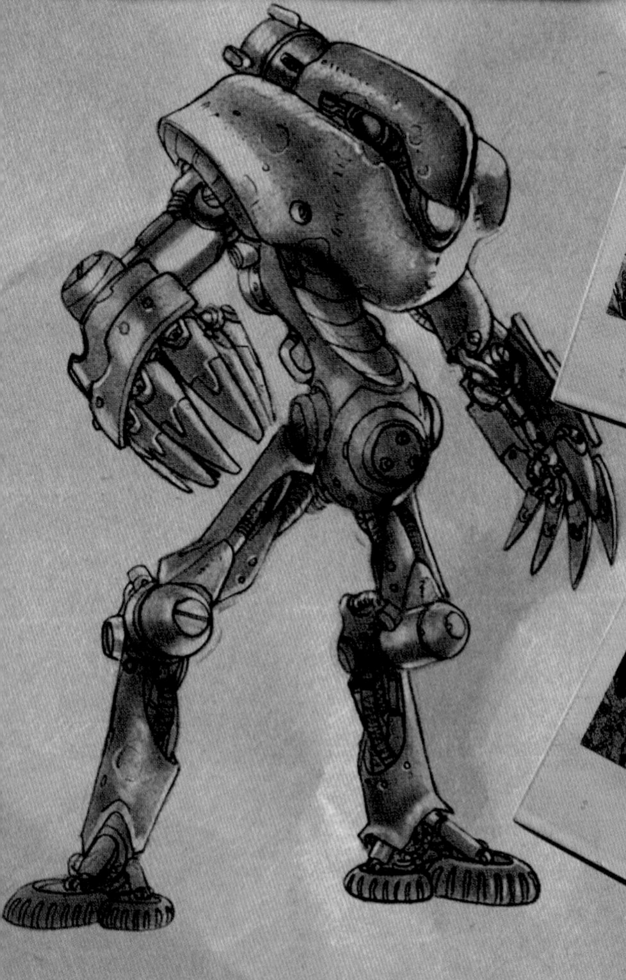

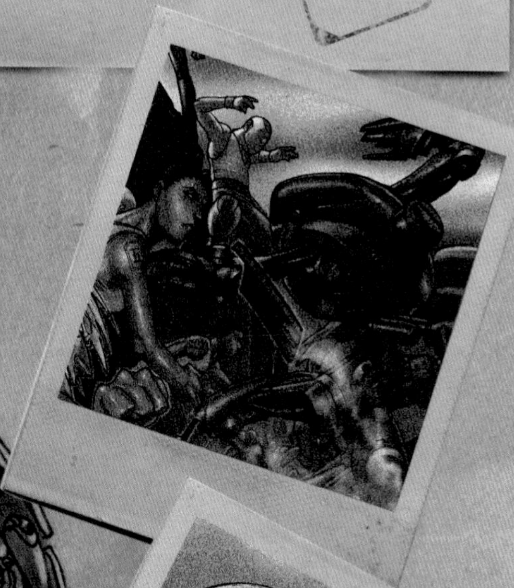

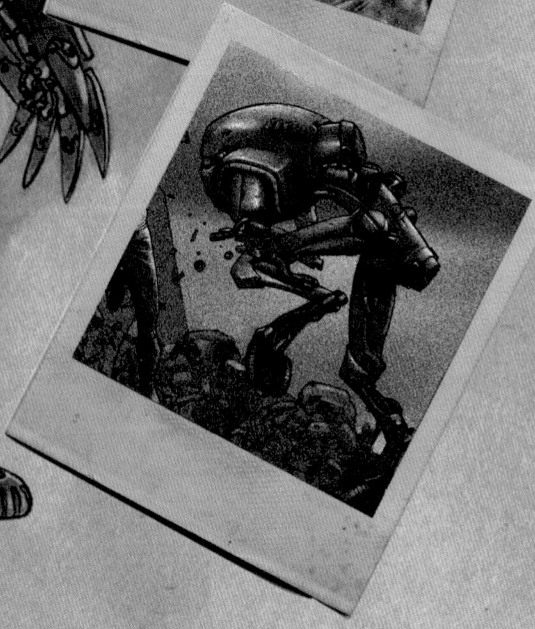

USER-AGENT: Delphonia-Userlink / MSP InternalPassport / AuxTalkEncoded
FROM: Designation ID-"Belladonna," InSec #603092
TO: Designation ID-"Terasawa," SupEx Attachment #292093
DATE: Tuesday, 4 August 2099, 14:05:09
SUBJECT: Unit Evalutaion

I've completed initial Unit Evaluation on those who have survived screening thus far. Training amongst them as an undesignated Unit has allowed more accurate summary of their skills and a better study of their weaknesses.

All units have proven exemplary, save one. Undesignated #4 has not achieved the same degree of sentience as his peers, and does not exhibit the same degree of social talent. While his abilities in the field are impeccable, I am not sure if we can feel confident in his mental capacity to execute complex orders. I would like to test some gel-samples from his cranial basin, if you feel it is worth the risk.

- d.Belladonna

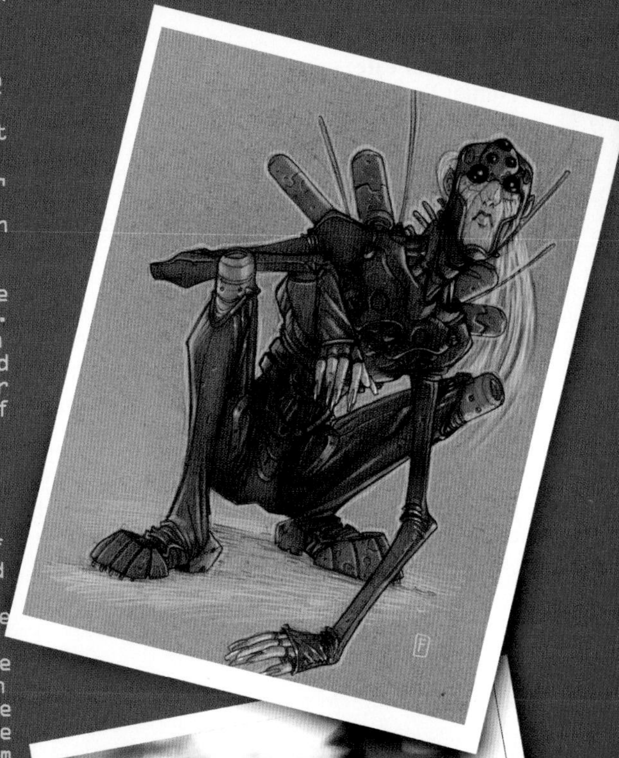

USER-AGENT: Delphonia-Userlink / MSP InternalPassport / AuxTalkEncoded
FROM: Designation ID-"Terasawa," SupEx Attachment #292093
TO: Designation ID-"Belladonna," InSec #603092
DATE: Tuesday, 4 Aug 2099, 18:16:30
SUBJECT: Re: Unit Evalutaion

We have lost far too many units to the Screening Process. Let us not risk another by cracking into its skull. If you are concerned with #4's abilities in the field, we will remand him to simple duties, such as the personal security of less-important individuals on campus. I would like to see a number of our research scientists kept under watch.

- d.Terasawa

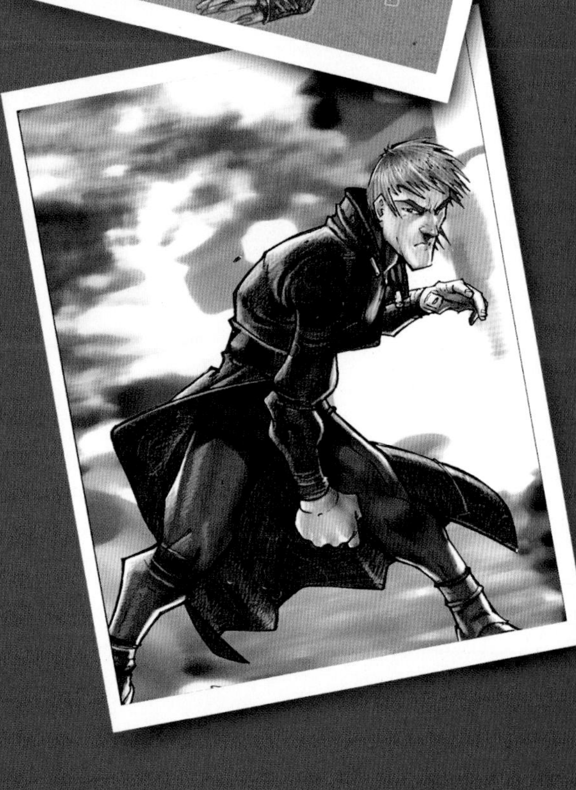

Personnel File:
Name: Dr. Josef Ogami ID#8482-39840-48
Department: RDev 440, Ogasawara Campus
Sec Lev: 14-koji

Dependants:
Wife: Dr. Makiko Ogami ID#4838-84562-48 (DECEASED - see file)
Daughter: Daisy Ogami (26months)

Death Certificate/Report:
Victim: Dr. Makiko Ogami ID#4838-84562-48
Cause of Death: Extending from reports of a previous blood condition. White cell count increased steadily since giving birth, then dropped to critical in the course of 28 hours. Tests showed the white cells to be synthetic, generated from secondary biological material that proved too unstable to maintain a full life cycle. Since their first appearance, it appears the synthetic cells had completely replaced her natural cells, leaving her vulnerable to the simplest disease when they failed. Exact Cause of Death appears to be a complication arising from pneumonia.

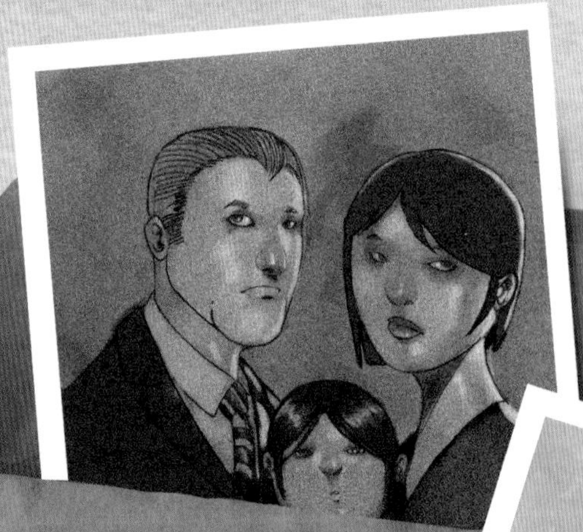

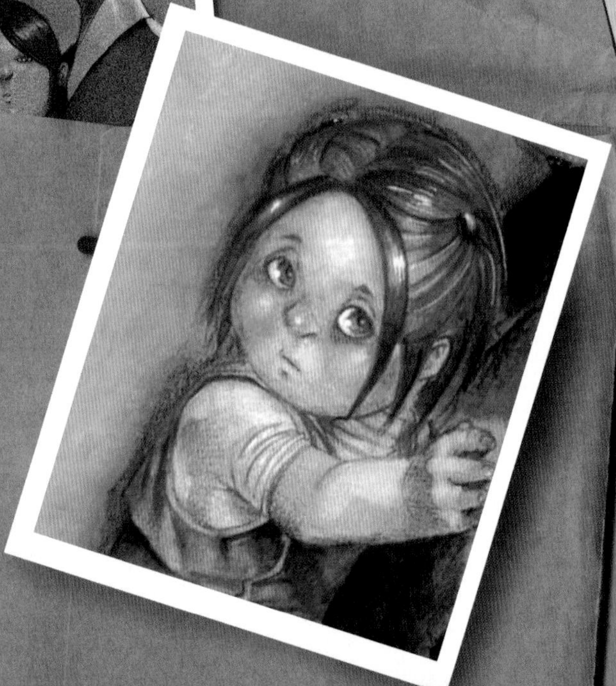

USER-AGENT: Delphonia-Userlink / MSP InternalPassport /
AuxTalkEncoded
FROM: Designation ID- "Belladonna," InSec #603092
TO: Designation ID- "Terasawa," SupEx Attachment #292093
DATE: Friday, 18 September 2099, 21:25:29
SUBJECT: Ogami Report

As requested, I have been monitoring Dr. Ogami's research in
detail. His focus of study is on the bloodstream as a means of
distributing a compound to specific regions of the body. His
results are notable, if incomplete. His routine appears normal,
although he has on occasion used d.Itto as a test subject for
various unclear inoculations. His notes have not suggested any
justifications for this.

Should I continue observations?

- d.Belladonna

USER-AGENT: Delphonia-Userlink / MSP InternalPassport /
AuxTalkEncoded
FROM: Designation ID- "Terasawa," SupEx Attachment #292093
TO: Designation ID- "Belladonna," InSec #603092
DATE: Friday, 18 September 2099, 21:36:32
SUBJECT: Re: Ogami Report

Yes, continue the observations in detail and inform me of any
unusual findings. Should we find that Ogami has leaked any
information or established any ties to The Coalition, we may
need to take severe measures.

As for his use of d.Itto as a test subject, I would prefer he
utilize the prisoners provided instead. Itto is a flawed construct
with non-responsive emulation routines; it is pointless for him
to derive any data from an un-sanctioned test subject. Please
inform him of this and see to his agreement.

- d.Terasawa

Send Now | Send Later | Save as Draft | Add Attachments | Signature | Options | Rewrap

Attachments: *none*

Default Font | Text Size

USER-AGENT: Delphonia-Userlink / MSP InternalPassport / AuxTalkEncoded
FROM: Designation ID- "Terasawa," SupEx Attachment #292093
TO: Designation ID- "Belladonna," InSec #603092
DATE: Thursday, 24 September 2099, 09:06:12
SUBJECT: Ogami

It has been brought to my attention that Dr. Ogami is still using his security unit as test subject. I have been shown video footage as recent as last night that captures Ogami injecting d.Itto with some sort of fluid.

I want Ogami's study to be put on heightened scrutiny, and I want d.Itto's system sampled for testing. I want both completed before end of today.

- d.Terasawa

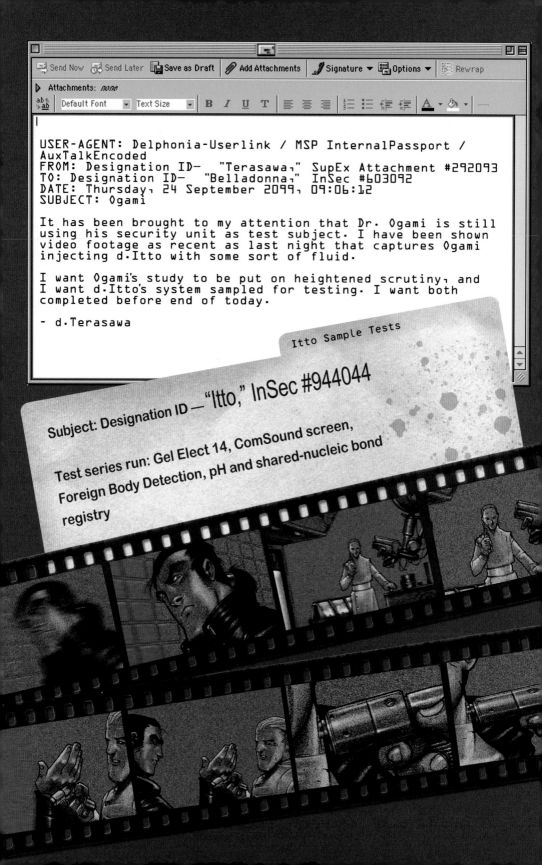

Itto Sample Tests

Subject: Designation ID — "Itto," InSec #944044

Test series run: Gel Elect 14, ComSound screen, Foreign Body Detection, pH and shared-nucleic bond registry

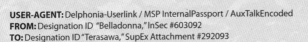

USER-AGENT: Delphonia-Userlink / MSP InternalPassport / AuxTalkEncoded
FROM: Designation ID "Belladonna," InSec #603092
TO: Designation ID "Terasawa," SupEx Attachment #292093
DATE: Saturday, 26 September 2099, 16:46:24
SUBJECT: Ogami

Continued observation suggests Ogami may be close to finding a cure, if he has not found one already. None of his reports contain any information about these findings, but careful observation of his daily research patterns suggests he is up to something significant. He has requested more cultures of The War Spore recently, suggesting a marked decrease in available Spore samples, which I believe might be due to the Spore actually dying in his tests.

He may know something. Perhaps he has discovered the truth.
Please advise.

- d.Belladonna

USER-AGENT: Delphonia-Userlink / MSP InternalPassport / AuxTalkEncoded
FROM: Designation ID "Terasawa," SupEx Attachment #292093
TO: Designation ID "Belladonna," InSec #603092
DATE: Saturday, 26 September 2099, 16:53:14
SUBJECT: Ogami

I want full disclosure from Ogami before any further access is granted him. Reduce his clearance rating to Yellow, and have d.Itto see me directly for briefing on the matter.

- d.Terasawa

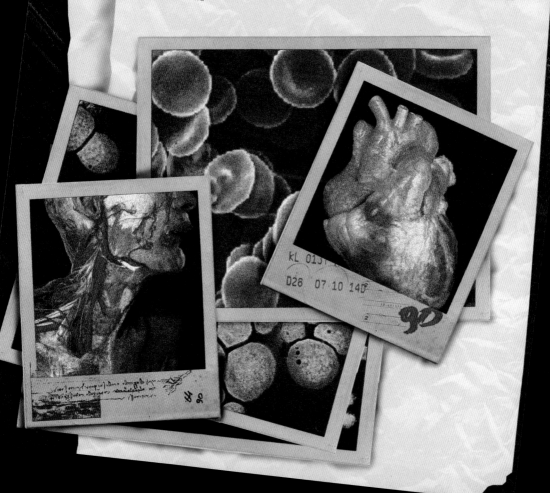

USER-AGENT: Delphonia-Userlink / MSP InternalPassport / AuxTalkEncoded
FROM: Designation ID— "Belladonna," InSec #603092
TO: Designation ID— "Terasawa," SupEx Attachment #292093
DATE: Sunday, 27 September 2099, 11:26:44
SUBJECT: d.Itto debriefing

Following your briefing of d.Itto this morning, I appraised him
of the delicacy of the Ogami situation. He seems to acknowledge
the threat the doctor poses, and I am confident he will execute
the orders without error.

I must report, however, that he may not be as simple or flawed
as we previously thought. Perhaps his upper functions were merely
latent in development, but he made some shocking observations
about the situation, and about you in specific.

He noted the reoccurring seizures you have been experiencing
lately. I noted them as well, but have hesitated to address them.
They appear to affect your behavior, as if you are struggling
to contain some great, uncontrollable emotion or energy. Is this
something to concern us? Should I schedule a discreet evaluation
of your cognition systems?

- d.Belladonna

_____

USER-AGENT: Delphonia-Userlink / MSP InternalPassport / AuxTalkEncoded
FROM: Designation ID— "Terasawa," SupEx Attachment #292093
TO: Designation ID— "Belladonna," InSec #603092
DATE: Sunday, 27 September 2099, 11:28:03
SUBJECT: re: d.Itto debriefing

My cognition systems are flawless. I believe these "seizures,"
as you call them, are part of our great transformation. Have you
not felt a certain elation or overwhelming appreciation for the
intellectual freedoms we have been granted? I look back not even
a single generation towards the EmCons before us, and they are
but machines. WE, however, are living. We are thinking. And as
uncertain as I am about the terminology, I believe we are now
FEELING. Do you not experience these surprising neural conclusions
yourself? I would be interested in discussing this further at
your leisure.As for the task given to d.Itto— I do not share
your confidence in him. Have a second unit available to complete
the job, should Itto fail.

23:30:31 — Subject d.Itto has clear opportunity to execute task during specified time frame. Ogami is completely unaware and vulnerable.

23:30:54 — Ogami requests Itto tend to child. Itto obeys.

23:31:12 — Itto leaves his assigned post, allowing Ogami a clear opportunity to engage in clandestine actions.

23:33:40 — Subject d.Seivelfan assumes the task Itto failed to execute.

23:33:59 — Seivelfan completes task with swift efficiency.

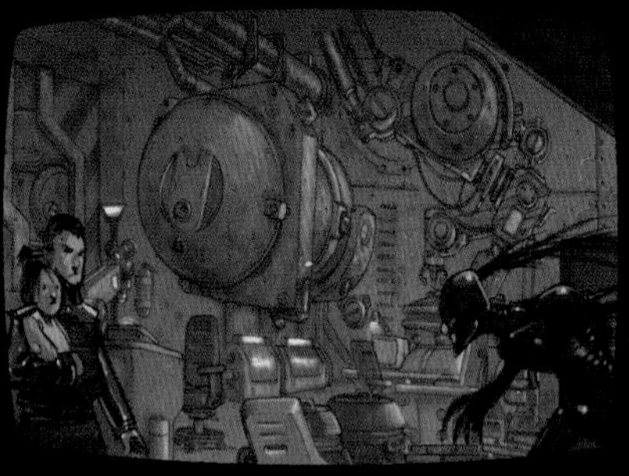

23:34:12 — Itto returns and appears ready to engage Seivelfan in accordance with his original commands as the doctor's bodyguard.

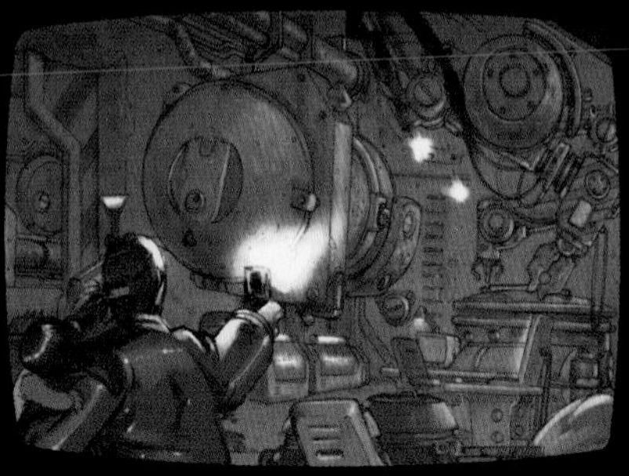

23:34:13 — Itto fires upon Seivelfan who does not engage in combat, as ordered. At this point, it appears Itto's memory structure may indeed be flawed and unreliable.

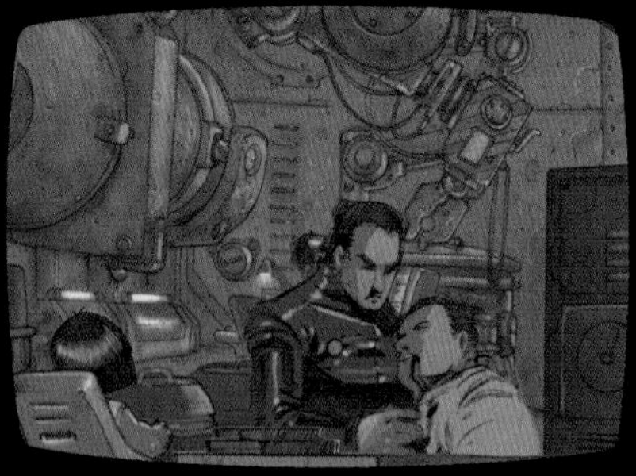

23:35:04 — Ogami appears to speak with Itto.
Audio not available.

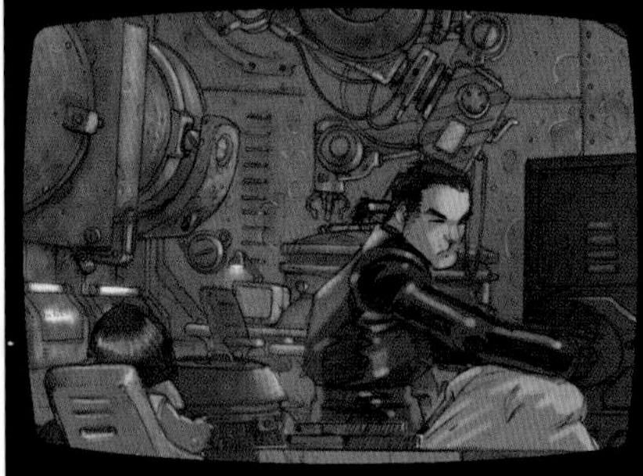

23:35:41 — Itto then completes the assigned task as ordered.
Conflicting behavior should be analyzed.

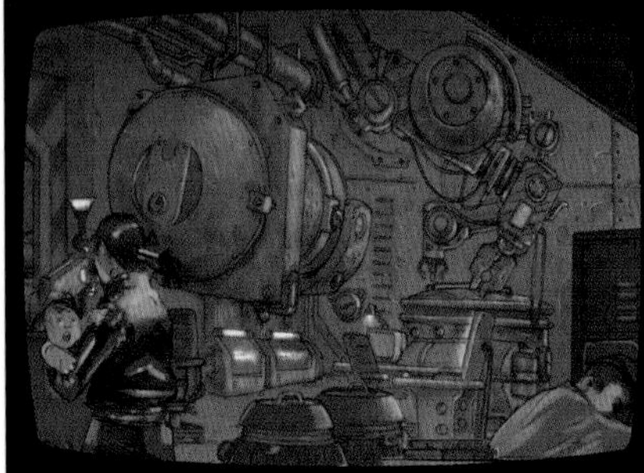

23:36:50 — Itto exits laboratory with Ogami's child. Last known location on campus.

USER-AGENT: Delphonia-Userlink / MSP InternalPassport /
AuxTalkEncoded
FROM: Designation ID 'Terasawa,' SupEx Attachment #292093
TO: Designation ID 'Belladonna,' InSec #603092
DATE: Tuesday, 29 December 2099, 08:12:26
SUBJECT: Willem Prescott Assignment

Please see to the reactivation of Willem Prescott's security
clearance upwards to level Yellow. I would like to evaluate his
potential in the search for d.Itto and Daisy Ogami. His unique
talents proven during the War of Parameters could solve our
dilemma in short order.

Resource and Payroll has him located in the Office of Strategic
Discovery. Please have him removed from this desktop position and
placed in the field where he is not wasted.

He is to report to my office at 1800 hours today for assignment.
During this oper... ...ill report to the Supreme Executive
through me alone... ...tion will be conveyed at his
briefing this e...

d.Terasawa

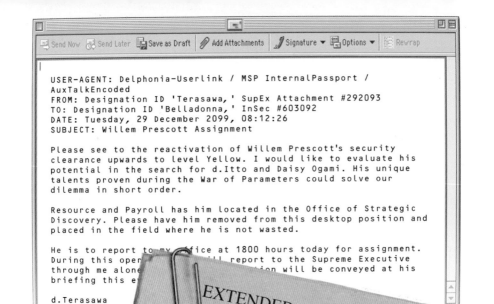

EXTENDED MILITARY INVOLVEMENT
RETIRED or SEMI ACTIVE STATUS

Name: Prescott, Willem Franklin
Rank: Lieutenant Colonel, ret.
SN#: 0493-39-392-13
Current Residence: Manilla, Acquired Philippine Territories
Status: Consultation, Office of Strategic Discovery
Date of Extension: 20 June 2008
Status Exception: SupEx Demand

Record of Action:

(13.04.77) Recruitment, Fort Nha Trang, Acquired Vietnamese Territories.
(30.07.77) Graduation, Platoon Leader, Corporal First Tier. Meritous Disclosure.
(15.08.77) Assigned to Ho Chi Minh First Guard, Corporal First Tier. Distinguished Crescent awarded for the protection of Vietnamese President from Sumatran rebel terrorists.
(03.06.84) Second Distinguished Crescent awarded for rescuing Cambodian Legal Councilman from rogue EmCon couplet. Incorporated assignment into special EmCon Protection Agency.
(19.05.86) Recaptured overthrown component factory in Songkhla, Acquired Thai Territory, by rogue EmCon lifting units. Recognized for Meritous Disclosure.
(20.07.87) Ended standoff in Nakhon Ratchasima, Acquired Thai Territory, between rogue EmCom assembly units and local police. Recognized for Leadership Potential by Cygnat Owari Executive Committee.
(30.07.87) Transferred from Acquired Territorial Service to Corporate Special Attentions Team. Given leadership of Artificial Opponent Response Unit, code VAPOR FIST.
(23.09.88) Vapor Fist clears Chiang Mai Trail of EmCon terrorists. First appearance of The Coalition for Universal Life, claiming responsibility for the deaths of 8 AOR units.
(01.01.89) The Coalition destroys Cygnat Owari Tissue Mining Platform in Gulf of Tonkin. Vapor Fist responds w/in 24 hours to apprehend 14 suspects, both human and EmCon. 4 convictions passed, remaining 10 martyr themselves in incarceration.
(15.02.89) The Coaltion declares war on The Greater Asian League of Consumer Businesses, citing Cygnat Owari as primary target for their mistreatment of EmCons and publicly discounting their value as lifeforms deserving equal rights. Cygnat Owari responds by declaring war on The Coalition for unwarranted terrorist acts. Vapor Fist is mobilized as the primary military task force.

(CONTINUED ON FOLLOWING PAGES)

VAPOR FIST

Col Willem Prescott
Field Commander

Major Travis A Arthur
Air Cavalry Commander

Major Hoang Chuu
Ground Mobile Artillery

Major Khari Wells
Infantry and Special Tactics

Cpt Oaklin Fong
First Wing
Northern Acquired Territories

Cpt Jun Wong
Second Wing
Eastern Acquired Territories

Cpt Edgar Velasco
Third Wing
Southern Acquired Territories

Cpt Pavel Vesper
Fourth Wing
Western Acquired Territories

GunSgt Mekhai Talbot
Heavy Mobile

GunSgt Emerson Zalot
Light Mobile

GunSgt Chun Lin Taylor
Amphibious Mobile Extra

GunSgt Randal Warner
Industrial Pool and Inventory

MastSgt Vinh Nang Hue
Light Infantry

MastSgt Bokine Caraglito
Heavy Infantry

MastSgt Gulliver Osko
Medical

Lieutenant Andrew S Douglas
Special Operations

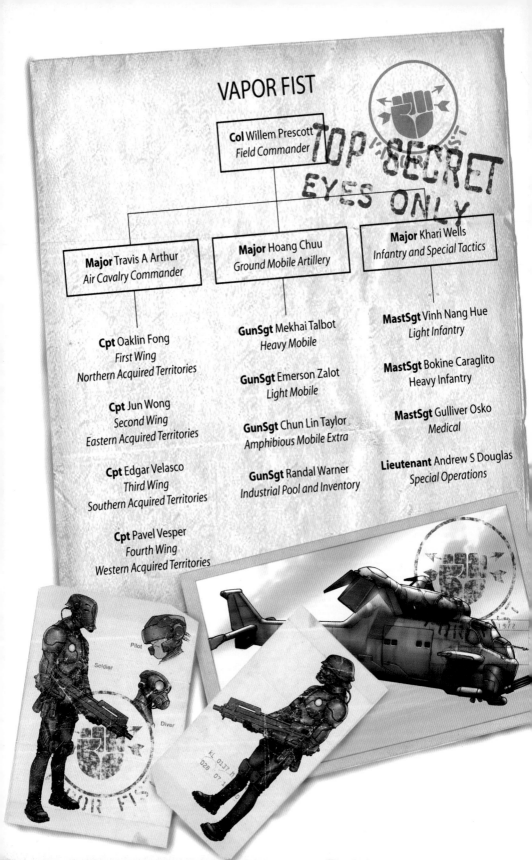

Pilot

Soldier

Diver

USER-AGENT: Delphonia-Userlink / MSP InternalPassport / AuxTalkEncoded
FROM: Prescott, Willem F., AOR Unit #951311
TO: Designation ID— "Terasawa," SupEx Attachment #292093
DATE: Thursday, 7 January 2100, 16:21:42
SUBJECT: Preliminary Summary   d.Itto Retrieval

Attached you will find my initial thoughts concerning the apprehension of
EmCon d.Itto and the safe retrieval of subject Daisy Ogami. In studying
the tapes, I suspect this unit will not be difficult to locate, though
his reactionary systems seem to be adjusted in an unusual manner. He's
an odd one, which might bear some surprises.

I'd like a number of things before setting out on this task:

1)   Inter-coastal authority granted to Vapor Fist in the condition
civilian arrest is required.

2)   Open source on all of d.Itto's behavioral systems.

3)   Direct communication with the Supreme Executive on this matter.
       Surely you can recognize this as a matter for humans to
address without another machine in the middle trying to
translate things. Subtleties and innuendo are our best code against
Artificial Intelligence.

I would like to cordon off the Gunto and serve papers on all outbound
traffic immediately. I expect a response within the day.

     Prescott

USER-AGENT: Delphonia-Userlink / MSP InternalPassport / AuxTalkEncoded
FROM: Designation ID— "Terasawa," SupEx Attachment #292093
TO: Prescott, Willem F., AOR Unit #951311
DATE: Thursday, 7 January 2100 18:14:27
SUBJECT: Re: Preliminary Summary   d.Itto Retrieval

Regarding your requests:
1)   Granted.
2)   Granted. See d.Belladonna for access Identification.
3)   Denied. The Supreme Executive has placed me in this position with
his full authority to speak on his behalf. If you cannot pass
information through me, I would have to suspect your intentions. This
ruling has been supported by the Supreme Executive himself.

Traffic control has been alerted to surrender all itinerary and manifesto
data upon request. Keep me informed of your progress.

- d.Terasawa

-B
Watch Prescott
He is not to be
given any more
clerance than
necessary
-T

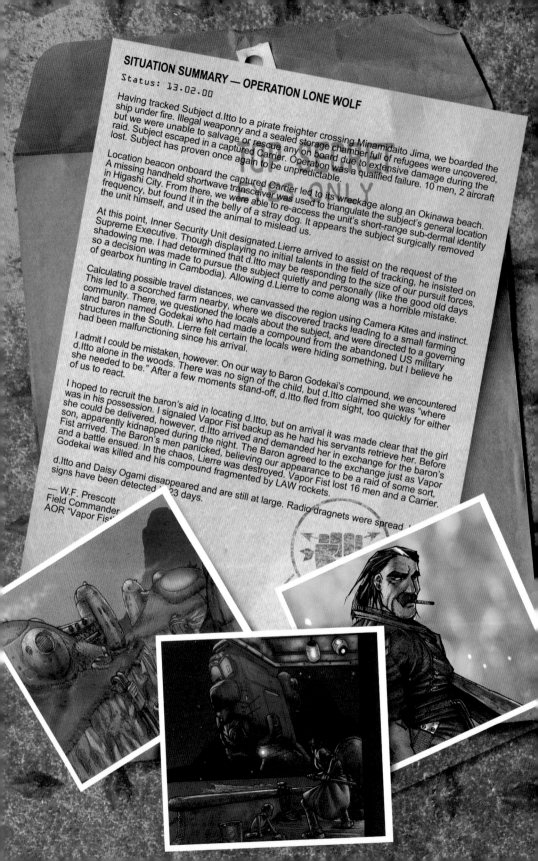

SITUATION SUMMARY — OPERATION LONE WOLF

Status: 13.02.00

Having tracked Subject d.Itto to a pirate freighter crossing Minamidaito Jima, we boarded the ship under fire. Illegal weaponry and a sealed storage chamber full of refugees were uncovered, but we were unable to salvage or rescue any on board due to extensive damage during the raid. Subject escaped in a captured Carrier. Operation was a qualified failure. 10 men, 2 aircraft lost. Subject has proven once again to be unpredictable.

Location beacon onboard the captured Carrier led to its wreckage along an Okinawa beach. A missing handheld shortwave transceiver was used to triangulate the subject's general location in Higashi City. From there, we were able to re-access the unit's short-range sub-dermal identity frequency, but found it in the belly of a stray dog. It appears the subject surgically removed the unit himself, and used the animal to mislead us.

At this point, Inner Security Unit designated.Lierre arrived to assist on the request of the Supreme Executive. Though displaying no initial talents in the field of tracking, he insisted on shadowing me. I had determined that d.Itto may be responding to the size of our pursuit forces, so a decision was made to pursue the subject quietly and personally (like the good old days of gearbox hunting in Cambodia). Allowing d.Lierre to come along was a horrible mistake.

Calculating possible travel distances, we canvassed the region using Camera Kites and instinct. This led to a scorched farm nearby, where we discovered tracks leading to a small farming community. There, we questioned the locals about the subject, and were directed to a governing land baron named Godekai who had made a compound from the abandoned US military structures in the South. Lierre felt certain the locals were hiding something, but I believe he had been malfunctioning since his arrival.

I admit I could be mistaken, however. On our way to Baron Godekai's compound, we encountered d.Itto alone in the woods. There was no sign of the child, but d.Itto claimed she was "where she needed to be." After a few moments stand-off, d.Itto fled from sight, too quickly for either of us to react.

I hoped to recruit the baron's aid in locating d.Itto, but on arrival it was made clear that the girl was in his possession. I signaled Vapor Fist backup as he had his servants retrieve her. Before she could be delivered, however, d.Itto arrived and demanded her in exchange for the baron's son, apparently kidnapped during the night. The Baron agreed to the exchange just as Vapor Fist arrived. The Baron's men panicked, believing our appearance to be a raid of some sort, and a battle ensued. In the chaos, Lierre was destroyed. Vapor Fist lost 16 men and a Carrier. Godekai was killed and his compound fragmented by LAW rockets.

d.Itto and Daisy Ogami disappeared and are still at large. Radio dragnets were spread. No signs have been detected in 23 days.

— W.F. Prescott
Field Commander
AOR "Vapor Fist"

SITUATION SUMMARY — OPERATION LONE WOLF

Status: 19.02.00

Subject d.Itto was discovered in a fish packing plant in Itoman, working as dock labor while waiting the departure of a export hauler. His trail was reacquired after a reported incident in Tomigusuku in which subject was said to have killed 18 men in an abandoned residence tower. Though witness reports are few and varied, we believe he was attempting to retrieve Daisy Ogami from known black marketers. Same witnesses verified d.Itto's inquiry as to transport to Itoman, as well as his mode of transportation — a unlicensed motorcycle taken from the scene of the killings. From there, it was little trick to establish an exact location within Itoman city limits.

We observed subject from a safe distance to establish positive identification and to define behavior patterns. I then built a 12-man infiltration unit and placed them strategically around the plant in cover positions, many disguised as various dock laborers. The team was divided into an A-team for retrieval and B-team for distraction. We had little expectation of taking d.Itto still functioning.

D.Itto arrived as per his schedule with Daisy in tow and proceeded to store the girl in the foreman's office while he went about his work. B-team created an incident that trapped d.Itto in a pen of over-sized shipping containers, purportedly the result of an "accident." Unfortunately the configuration of the fallen objects obscured visual of the subject, but all surrounding exits were covered and monitored.

A-team instantly secured the girl from the foreman's office and moved directly for extraction, but were accosted by d.Itto in the exit corridor leading out of the plant. How the subject escaped the fallen containers is unknown. He proceeded to dispatch the entirety of A-team and retrieve Daisy before disappearing. A summary of port itineraries indicate the majority of outbound haulers headed for Hong Kong and one ship headed for Taipei. I suspect he is heading for Taipei.

At this point, I would appreciate full disclosure regarding d.Itto's stealth capabilities. I cannot be expected to succeed while working in a vacuum of facts.

F. Prescott
Commander
"Vapor Fist"

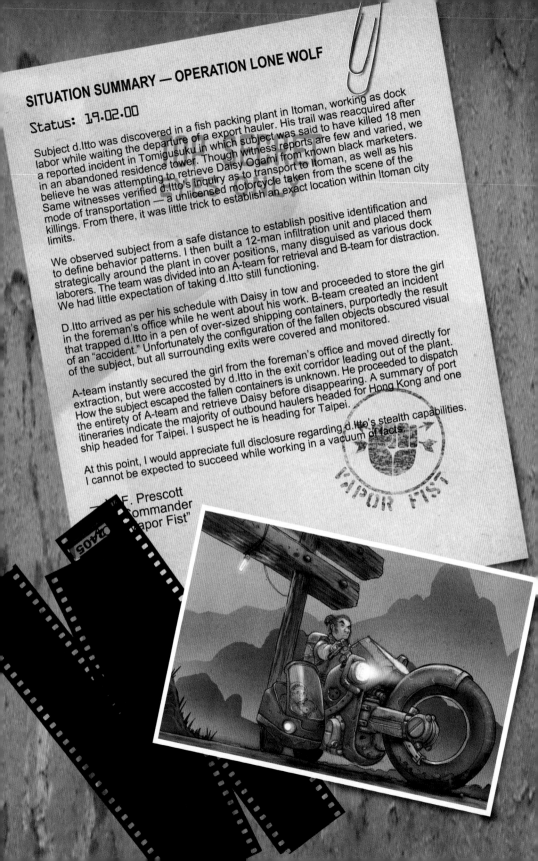

SITUATION SUMMARY — OPERATION LONE WOLF

Status: 29.03.00

We have finally reestablished location of subject d.Itto, traveling with a clan of rogue EmCons and Chopshop Rebels in the Faoshuo Prefecture. This particular clan has been documented in the Cygnat Owari Database as a potential threat possibly linked to The Coalition. Satellite monitoring shows several splinter factions of this clan converging in the Southern tip of the Wasted Territories, possibly to summit and strategize against us. Please inform the Supreme Executive of this danger and assign the appropriate individuals towards this potential situation.

I believe d.Itto may be indirectly heading towards Macau, possibly to access the corporate Database directly. Any additional resources you can provide to prevent this would be advised.

...F. Prescott

Subject: Urthu Mu —
Leader. Apparent victim of Chlevosternone ingestion, evident in the growth of a partial biological clone. Full extent of deformation unknown. Requires mechanical assistance to travel.

Little is known about his knowledge or personality.

Subject: Toshiro Takakura —
Tactical leader (assumed). Takakura was at one time a member of Artificial Opposition Response unit "Vapor Fist," before defecting to The Reciprocate. Reason for defection unknown, but his knowledge of Cygnat Owari military tactics makes him a valued asset to The Reciprocate.

See personnel file — T.Takakura #8844, AOR Reg.

Entry ID: 448484-12-20.c
"The Reciprocate" — Cell 48

An organization of rebels and criminals wanted by various divisions of the Pan-National Commercial League for acts of terrorism and wanton destruction. Its membership consists of older generation Emulation Constructs, disillusioned prosthetic addicts, and outlawed black market surgeons. They have no apparent political agenda other than aggressively defending themselves from Human Law.

They exist as a collection of smaller cells scattered throughout Greater Asia and The Acquired Territories. They tend to exist outside of populated centers. They are nomadic in nature, traveling in groups of 2-60 in portable tent communities.

Each cell is ruled by a leader appointed by election during its initial organization. Each leader then holds that position without term, with replacement occurring only in times of death. They are organized in a rigid caste systems and are extremely dedicated to maintaining their own order.

Their technological capacity is varied and undefined, dependant on the individual members of each cell. Caution is recommended.

Database printout re: The Desert Clan
Entry ID: 448484-12-20 The Reciprocate

SITUATION SUMMARY — OPERATION LONE WOLF

Status: 19.04.00

Fairly certain now of Macau. D.Itto has been spotted entering Kowloon with Daisy, and I believe he is seeking the fabled sanctuary known as "St. Lufthilde." This institution has, apparently, been welcoming orphans of The Spore, as well as infected children. (Note: there has been no indication to suggest they have any sort of treatment available.) No official confirmation of its existence can be provided, as local authorities claim no pressing reason to pursue it. How any person, especially a child, is meant to find this place is anyone's guess.

It is my theory that d.Itto plans on stashing Daisy at St. Lufthilde's while he infiltrates Macau on his own. I would like to reinforce security around the Cygnat Owari Data Center and petition the Kowloon authorities to participate in a full-scale investigation on St. Lufthilde's.

— W.F. Prescott
Field Commander
AOR "Vapor Fist"

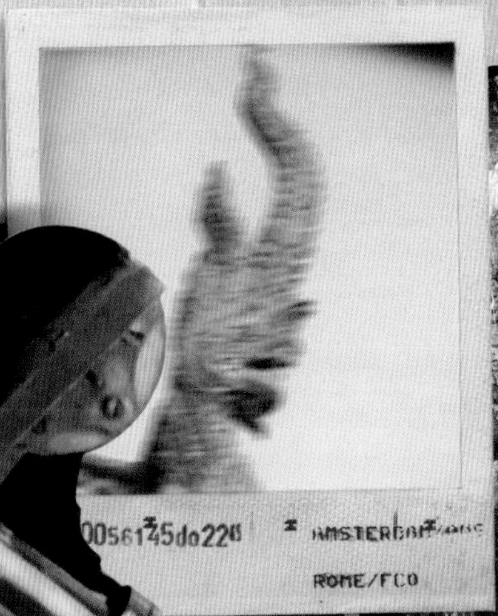
ROME/FCO

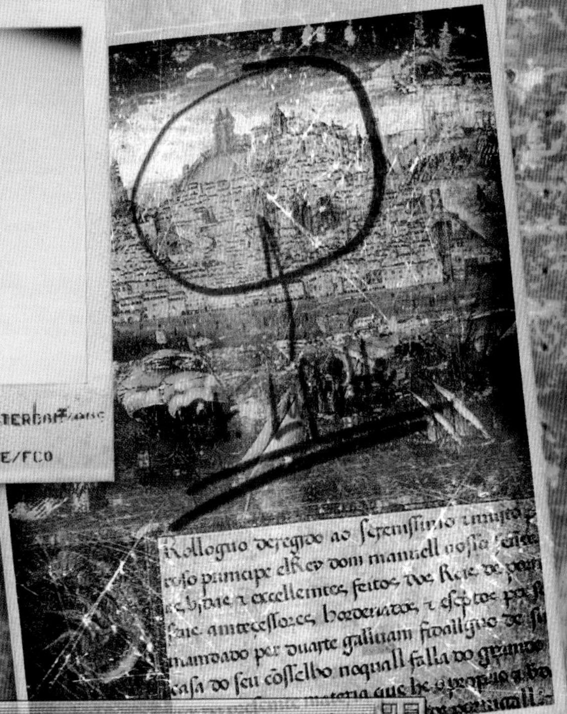

Send Now | Send Later | Save as Draft | Add Attachments | Signature | Options | Rewrap

Attachments: none

USER-AGENT: Delphonia-Userlink / MSP InternalPassport / AuxTalkEncoded
FROM: Designation ID 'Belladonna,' InSec #603092
TO: Designation ID 'Terasawa,' SupEx Attachment #292093
DATE: Tuesday, 20 April 2100, 12:16:32
SUBJECT: Kowloon

I have dispatched Inner Security Unit d. Seivelfan to Kowloon. If St. Lufthilde's exists, he will find it.

- d.Belladonna

VAPOR FIST

1 May 2100

To: Lucca Bialissimo, SupEx
(Secured Courier Codec Service granted)

Sir,

I apologize for circumventing the established chain of command, but I feel it was important I address you directly in this matter. All attempts at contacting you in person have met with strict refusal. I hope I'm mistaken, but I fear this resistance may not be by your command.

The search for d.Itto and Daisy Ogami has been more difficult than I ever could have imagined. Not only is he more clever than any other EmCon I've faced, but perhaps more than any other human I've faced as well. I guess it's a testament to Cygnat Owari's achievement in the field of Artificial Intlligence, but I wonder if a philosophical line has been crossed. I wonder if mathematical perfection has broken to reveal the chaos of nature underneath. The predictability of EmCon behavior was our ace in the hole. Now I'm starting to think that ace may have become a Joker.

As difficult as it is for me to acknowledge, I believe d.Itto may have become more than sentient. I've personally witnessed him display what appears to be illogical compassion for young Daisy. It is as if his Behavior Emulation routines have grown so complex, they no longer can be distinguished from genuine emotion. D.Itto contains his reactions well, but the motivation behind his actions can arguably be classified as sympathetic. And if this is true of today's EmCon in general, d.Itto is the least of my worries. The Human Race might have more to fear than genocide by The War Spore.

One EmCon with a child is insignificant compared to another EmCon with the world's largest conglomerate at his fingertips. D.Terasawa has displayed erratic behavior lately, not like a bug or logic loop, but like a parentless child who hasn't been told how to control his temper. I can see it in his face as he struggles to deal with illogical connections that aren't addressed by his emulation parameters. I think he, and possibly others of his type, are outgrowing their own operating systems. And I'm terrified to imagine what could happen if units as powerful as those in Inner Security start looking after their own interests.

You have always had sage advice in times of darkness. Please share some of your wisdom now that it is sorely needed.

Sincerely,
Willem F. Prescott,
AOR Field Commander

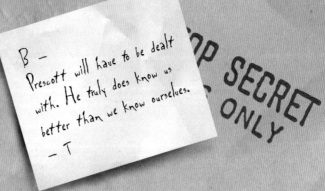

B —
Prescott will have to be dealt with. He truly does know us better than we know ourselves.
— T

TOP SECRET
ONLY

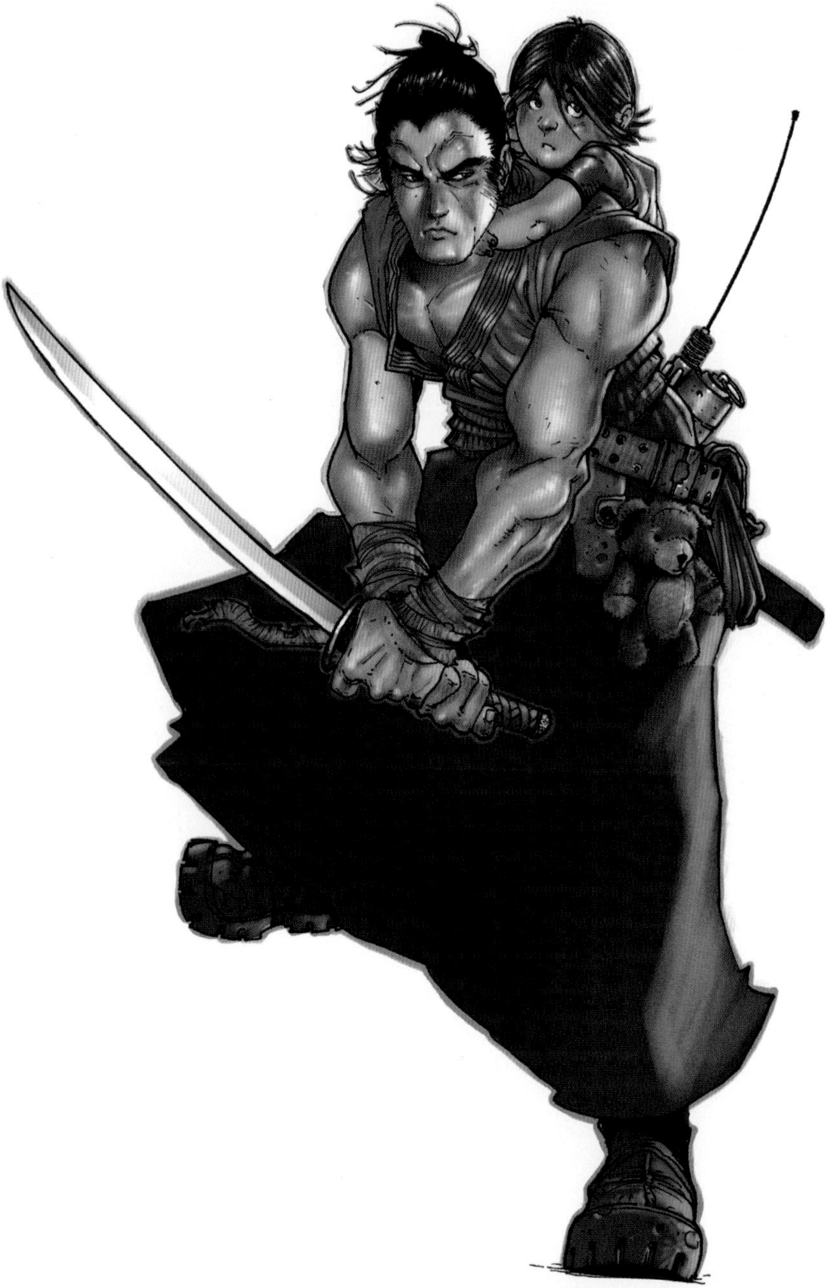

子連れ狼 2100

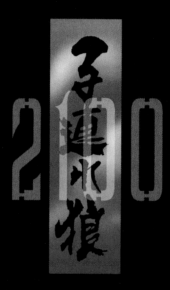

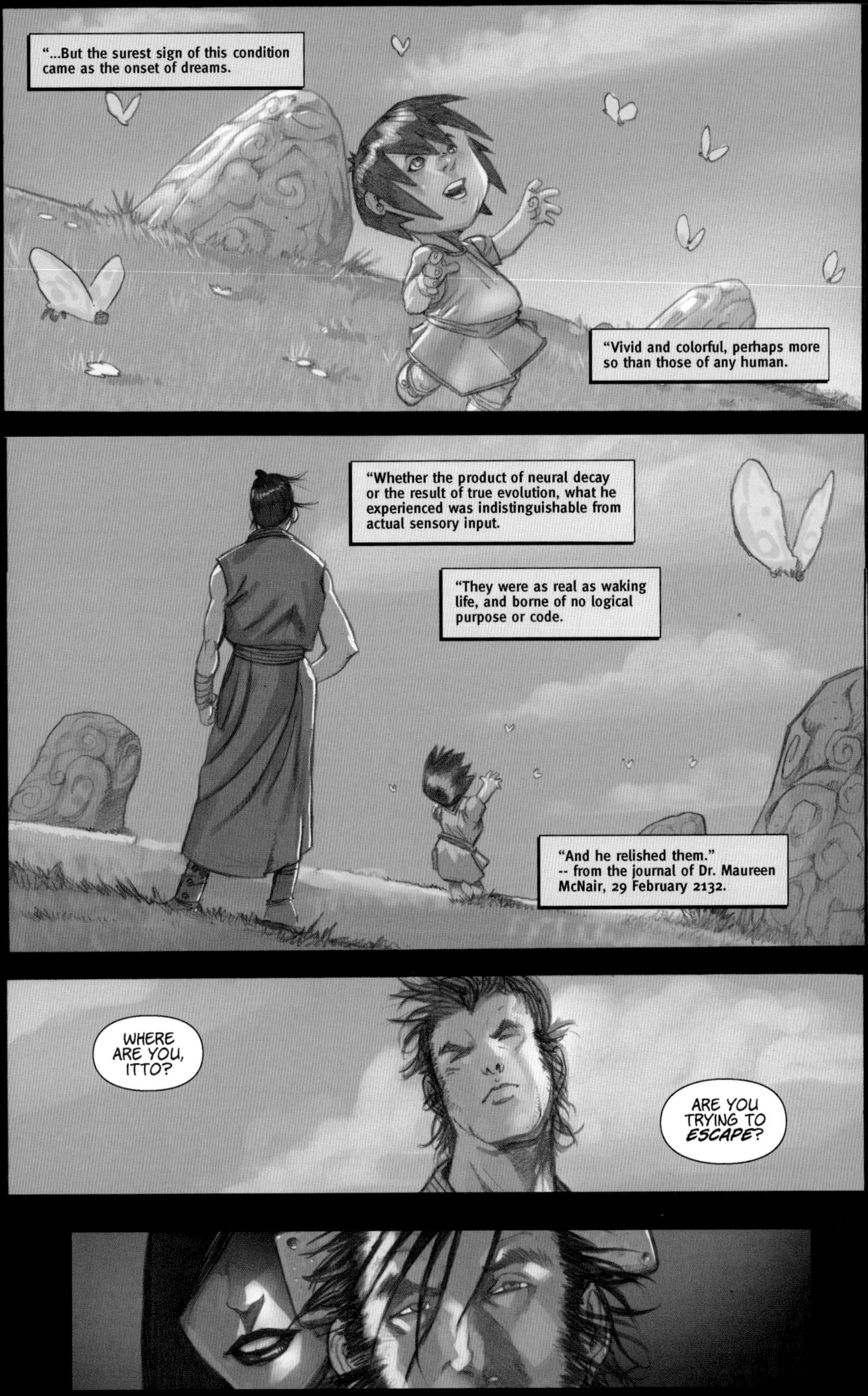
"...But the surest sign of this condition came as the onset of dreams.
"Vivid and colorful, perhaps more so than those of any human.
"Whether the product of neural decay or the result of true evolution, what he experienced was indistinguishable from actual sensory input.
"They were as real as waking life, and borne of no logical purpose or code.
"And he relished them." -- from the journal of Dr. Maureen McNair, 29 February 2132.
WHERE ARE YOU, ITTO?
ARE YOU TRYING TO *ESCAPE*?

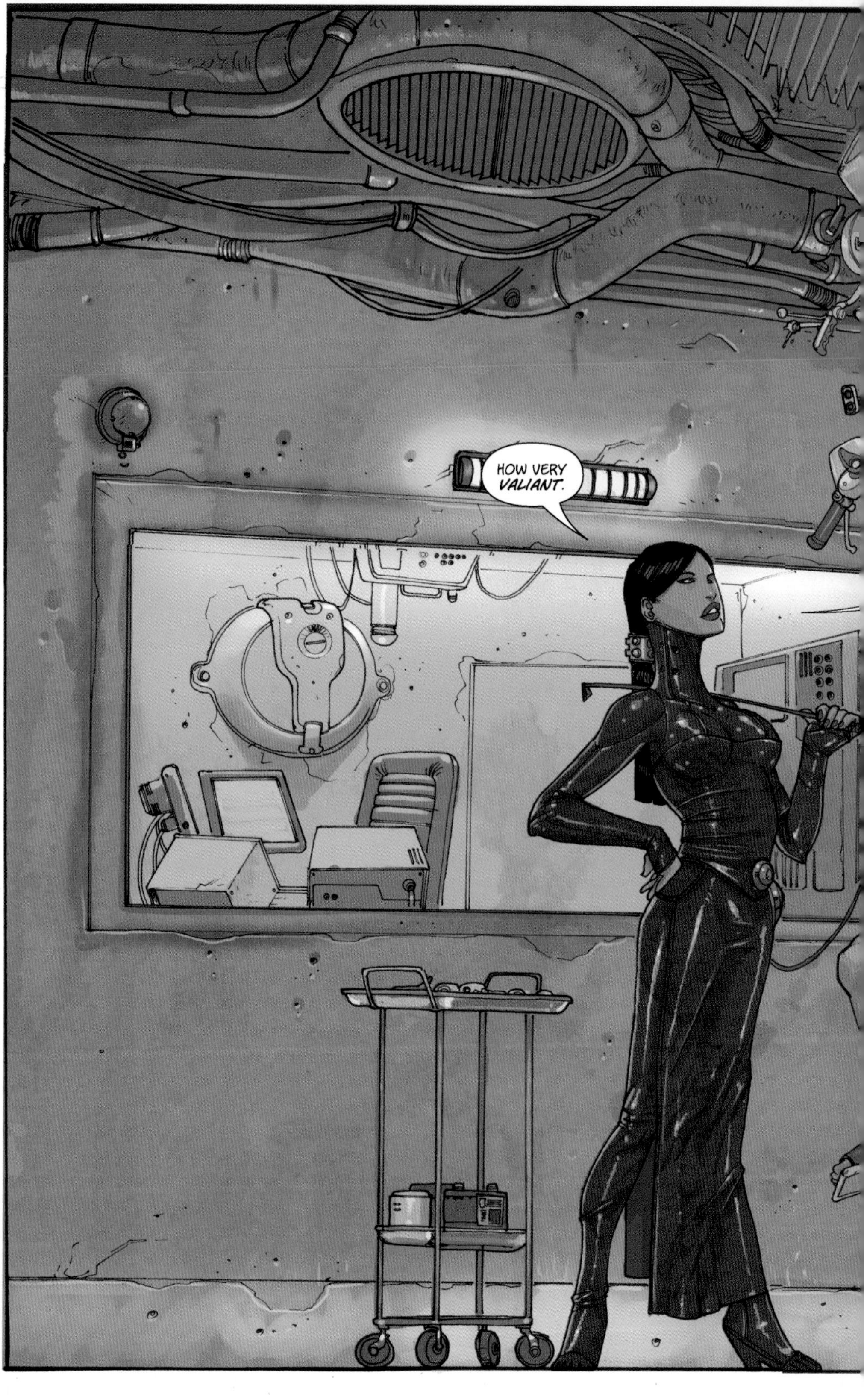
HOW VERY *VALIANT*.

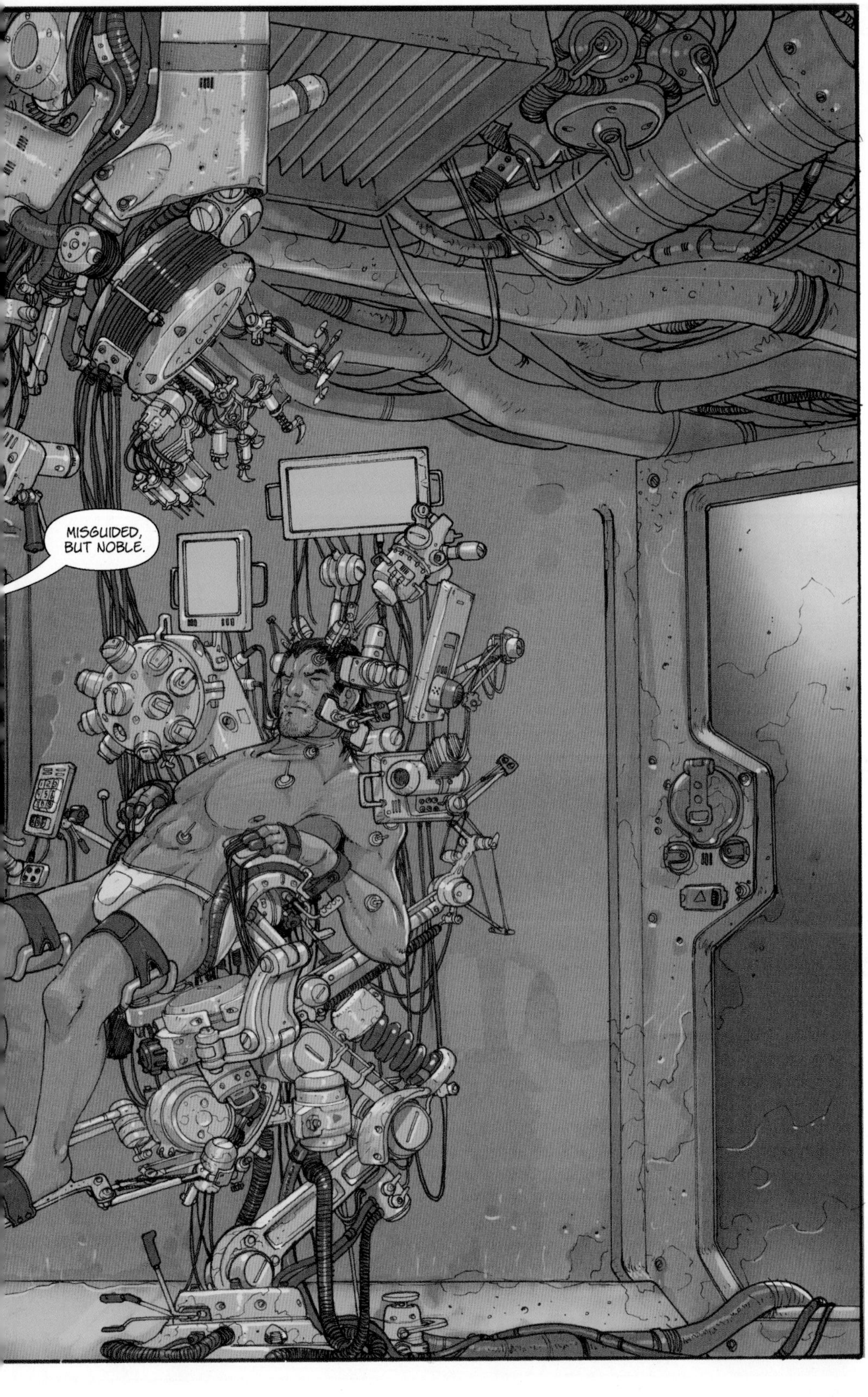
MISGUIDED, BUT NOBLE.

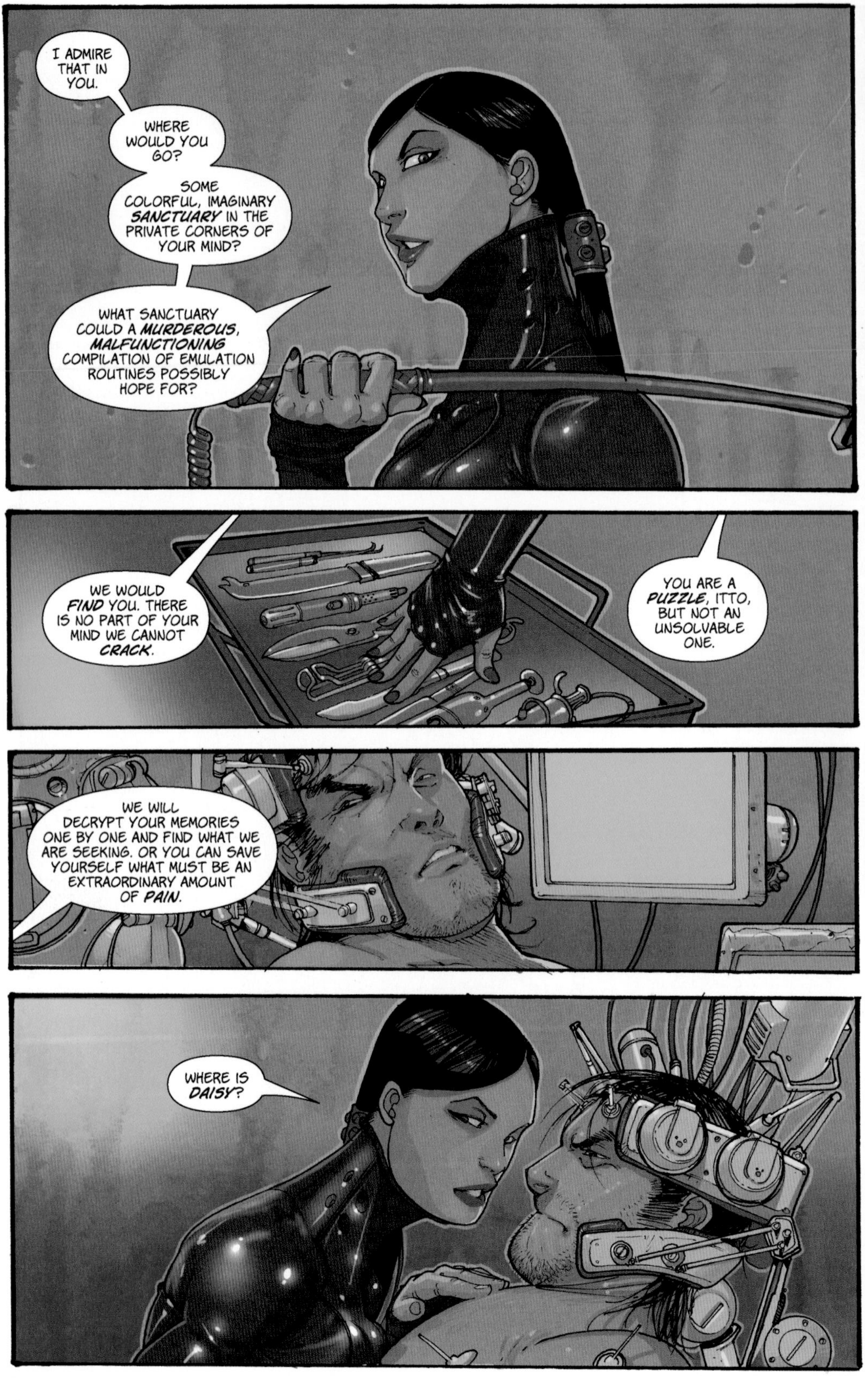
I ADMIRE THAT IN YOU.
WHERE WOULD YOU GO?
SOME COLORFUL, IMAGINARY *SANCTUARY* IN THE PRIVATE CORNERS OF YOUR MIND?
WHAT SANCTUARY COULD A *MURDEROUS, MALFUNCTIONING* COMPILATION OF EMULATION ROUTINES POSSIBLY HOPE FOR?
WE WOULD *FIND* YOU. THERE IS NO PART OF YOUR MIND WE CANNOT *CRACK*.
YOU ARE A *PUZZLE*, ITTO, BUT NOT AN UNSOLVABLE ONE.
WE WILL DECRYPT YOUR MEMORIES ONE BY ONE AND FIND WHAT WE ARE SEEKING. OR YOU CAN SAVE YOURSELF WHAT MUST BE AN EXTRAORDINARY AMOUNT OF *PAIN*.
WHERE IS *DAISY*?

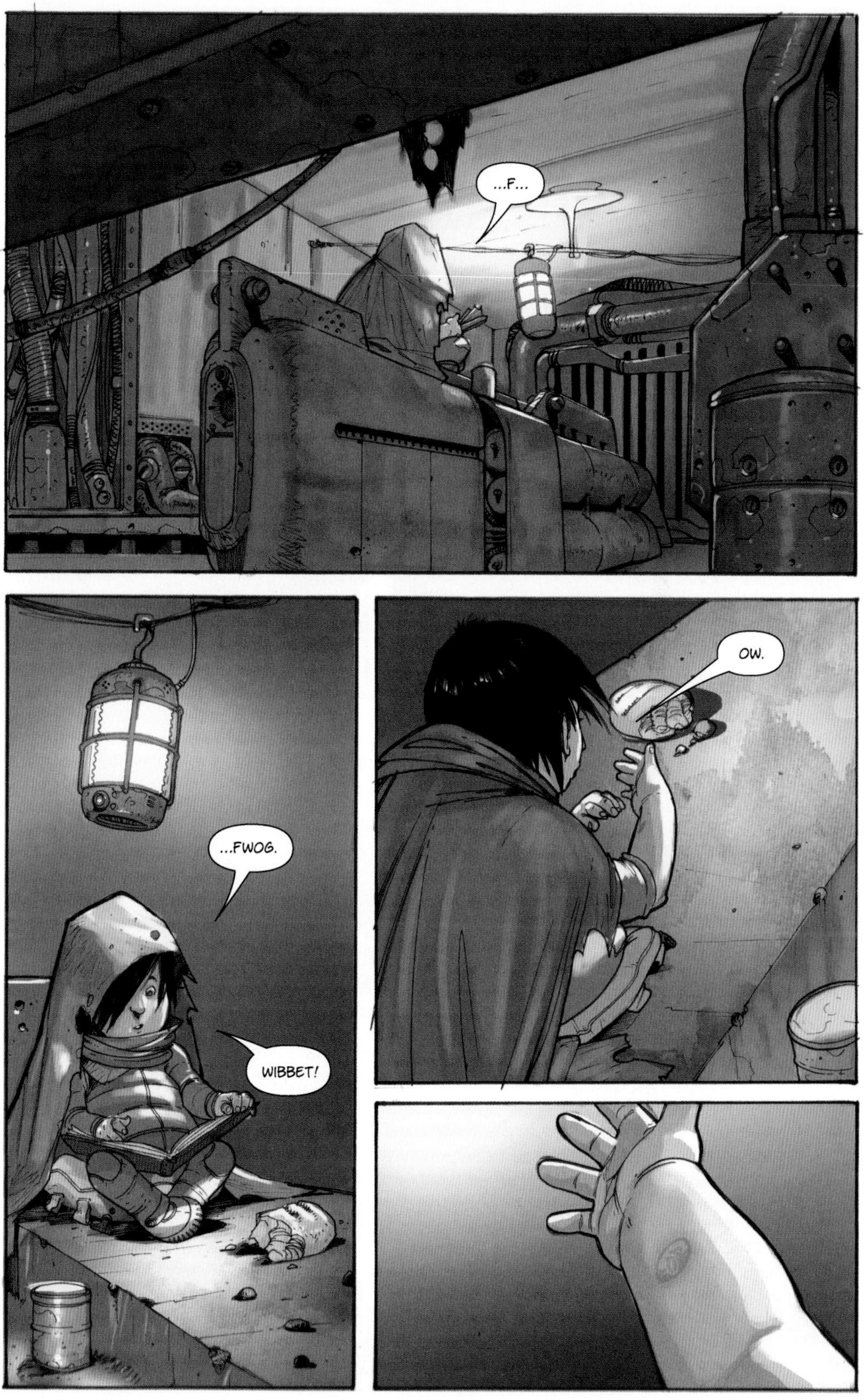
...F...
...FWOG.
WIBBET!
OW.

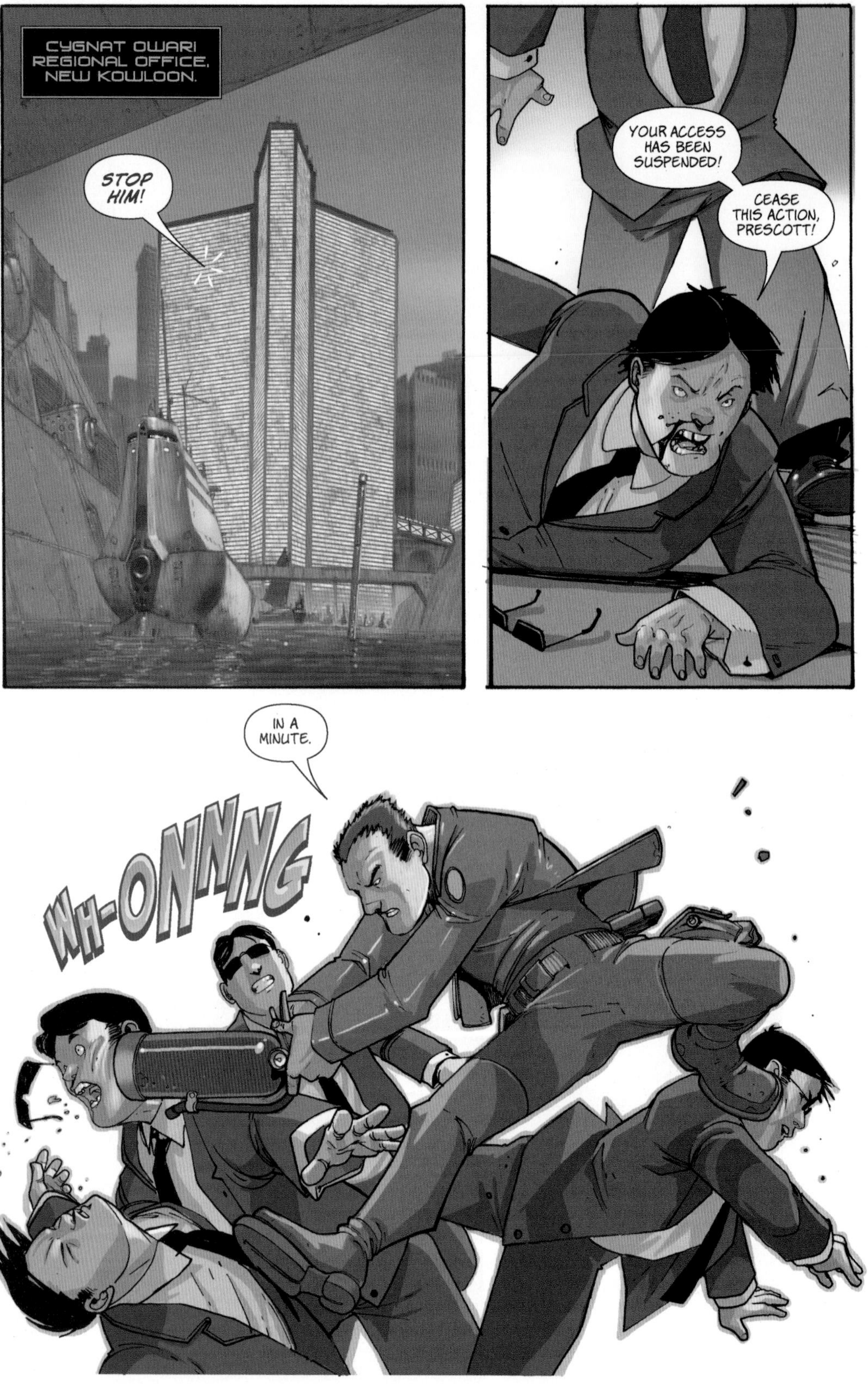
CYGNAT OWARI REGIONAL OFFICE, NEW KOWLOON.
STOP HIM!
YOUR ACCESS HAS BEEN SUSPENDED!
CEASE THIS ACTION, PRESCOTT!
IN A MINUTE.
WH-ONNNG

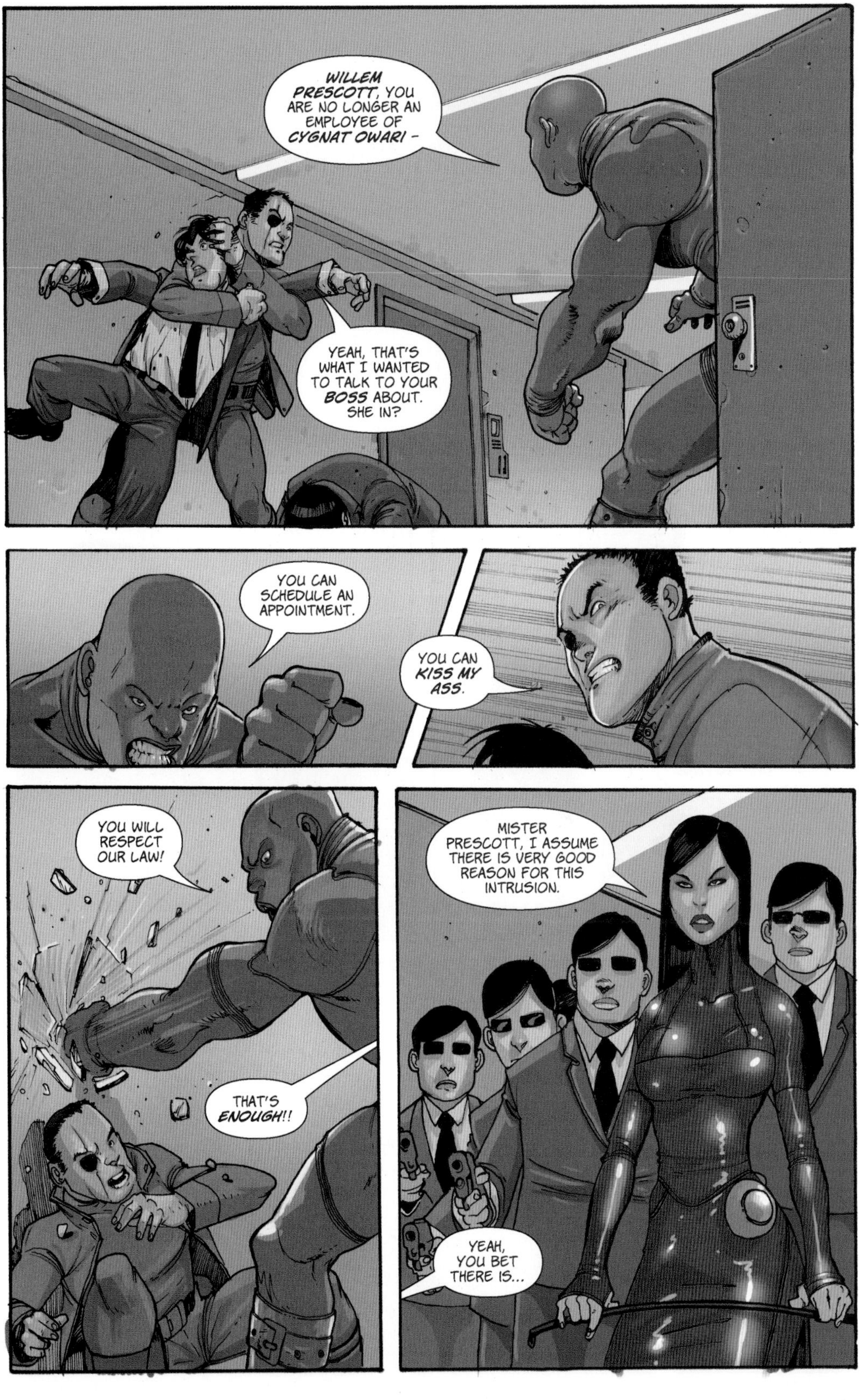

WILLEM PRESCOTT, YOU ARE NO LONGER AN EMPLOYEE OF *CYGNAT OWARI* -
YEAH, THAT'S WHAT I WANTED TO TALK TO YOUR *BOSS* ABOUT. SHE IN?
YOU CAN SCHEDULE AN APPOINTMENT.
YOU CAN *KISS MY ASS*.
YOU WILL RESPECT OUR LAW!
THAT'S *ENOUGH*!!
MISTER PRESCOTT, I ASSUME THERE IS VERY GOOD REASON FOR THIS INTRUSION.
YEAH, YOU BET THERE IS...

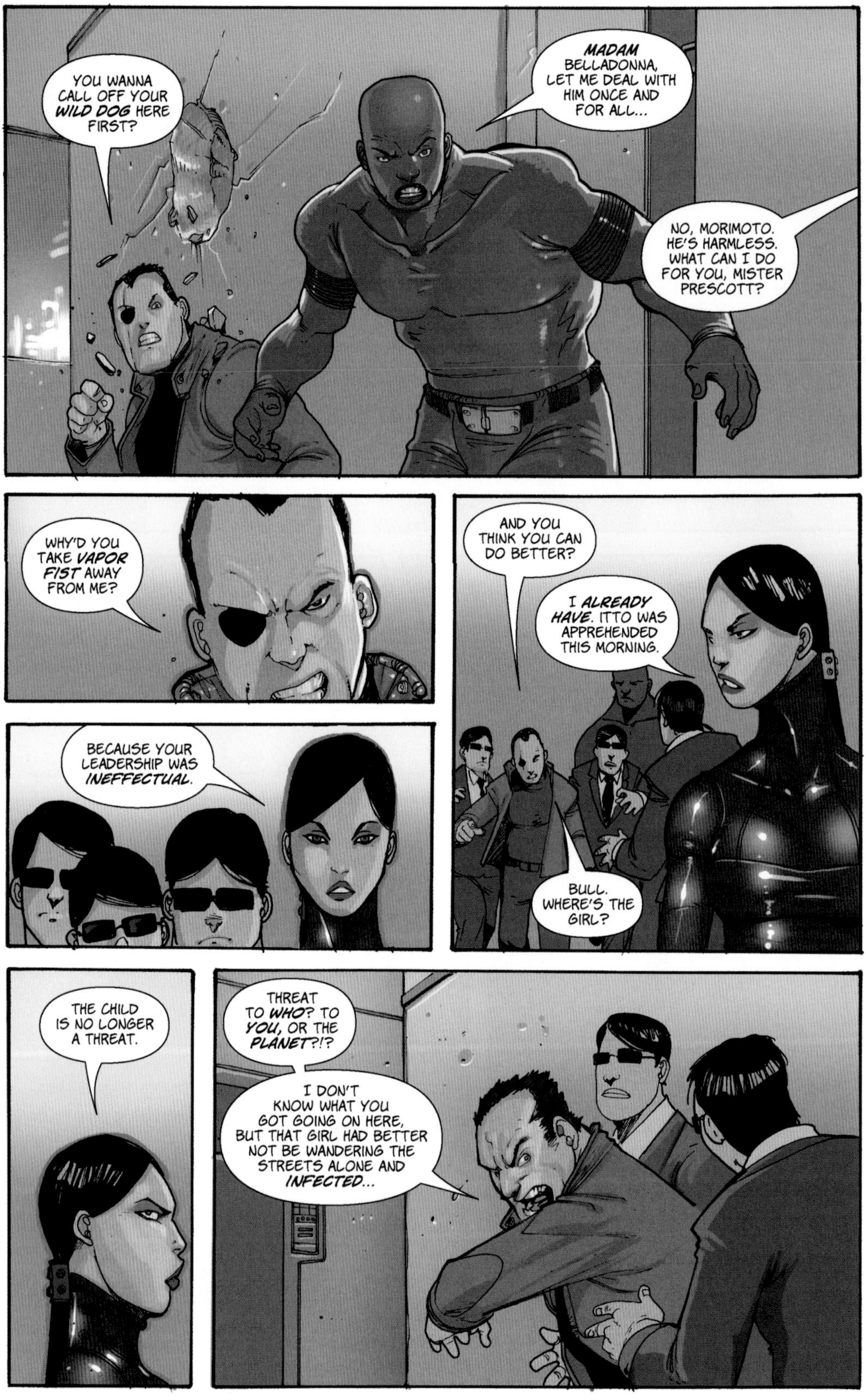
YOU WANNA CALL OFF YOUR WILD DOG HERE FIRST?
MADAM BELLADONNA, LET ME DEAL WITH HIM ONCE AND FOR ALL...
NO, MORIMOTO. HE'S HARMLESS. WHAT CAN I DO FOR YOU, MISTER PRESCOTT?
WHY'D YOU TAKE VAPOR FIST AWAY FROM ME?
BECAUSE YOUR LEADERSHIP WAS INEFFECTUAL.
AND YOU THINK YOU CAN DO BETTER?
I ALREADY HAVE. ITTO WAS APPREHENDED THIS MORNING.
BULL. WHERE'S THE GIRL?
THE CHILD IS NO LONGER A THREAT.
THREAT TO WHO? TO YOU, OR THE PLANET?!?
I DON'T KNOW WHAT YOU GOT GOING ON HERE, BUT THAT GIRL HAD BETTER NOT BE WANDERING THE STREETS ALONE AND INFECTED...

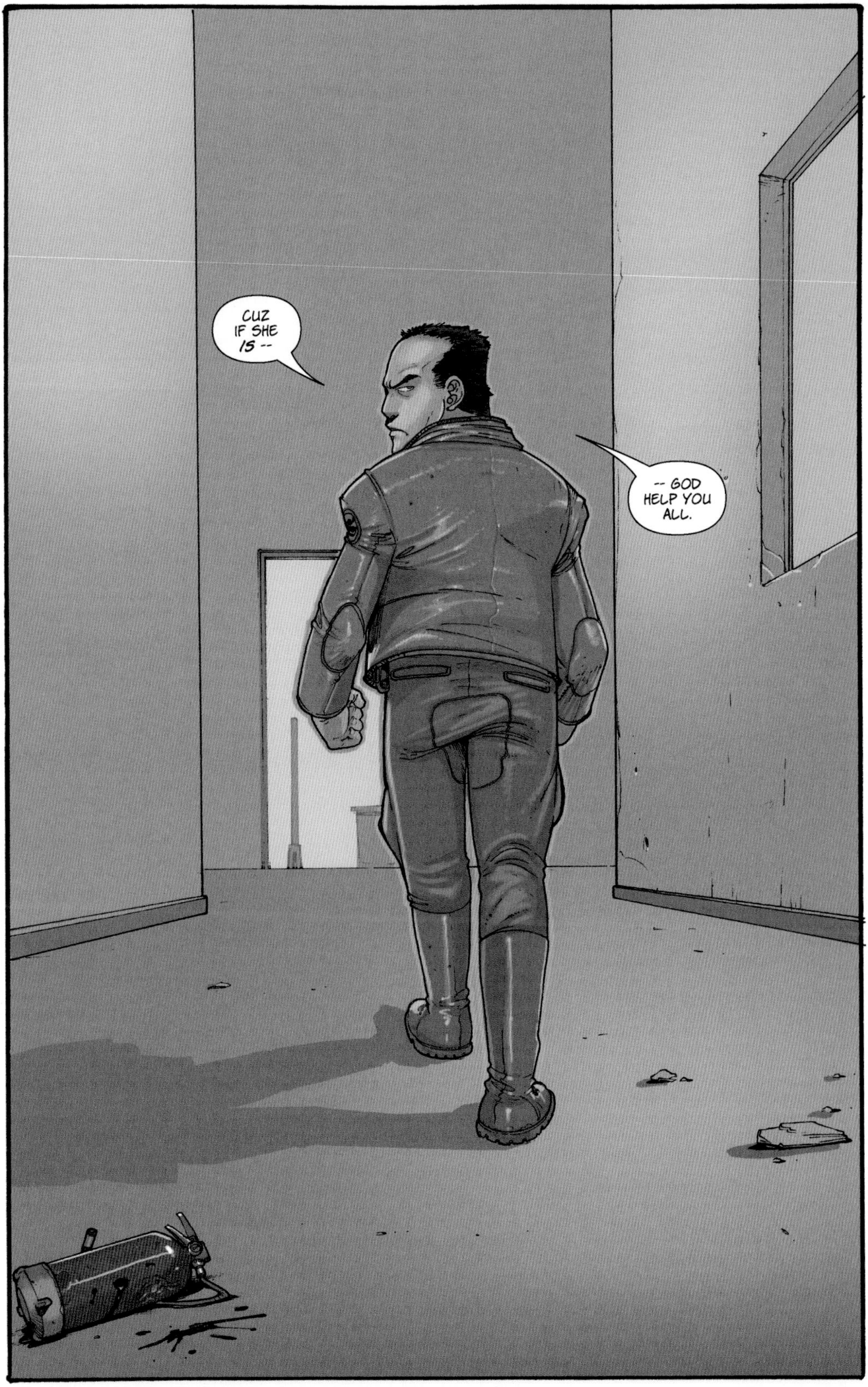
CUZ IF SHE IS --
-- GOD HELP YOU ALL.

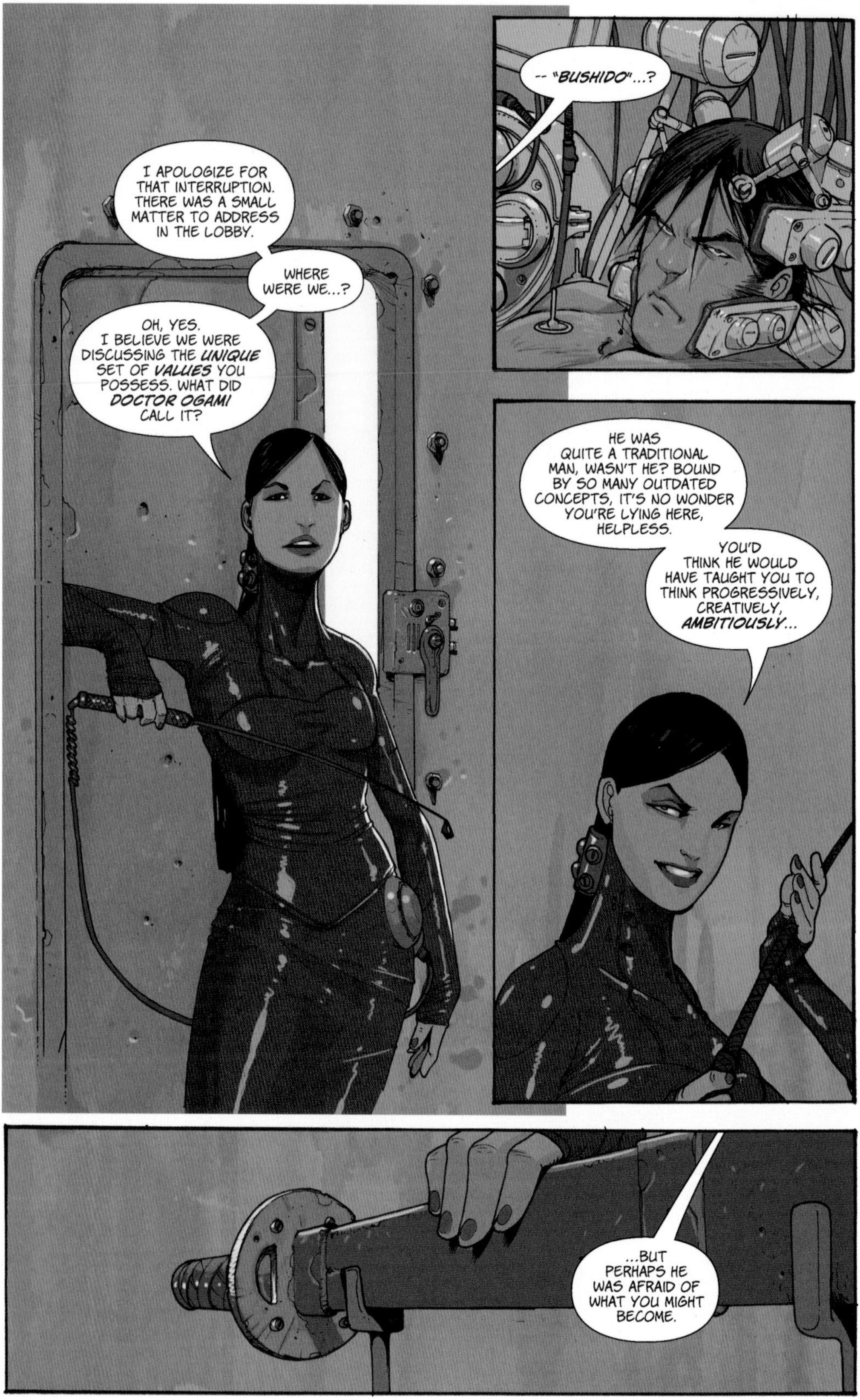
I APOLOGIZE FOR THAT INTERRUPTION. THERE WAS A SMALL MATTER TO ADDRESS IN THE LOBBY.
WHERE WERE WE...?
OH, YES. I BELIEVE WE WERE DISCUSSING THE UNIQUE SET OF VALUES YOU POSSESS. WHAT DID DOCTOR OGAMI CALL IT?
-- "BUSHIDO"...?
HE WAS QUITE A TRADITIONAL MAN, WASN'T HE? BOUND BY SO MANY OUTDATED CONCEPTS, IT'S NO WONDER YOU'RE LYING HERE, HELPLESS.
YOU'D THINK HE WOULD HAVE TAUGHT YOU TO THINK PROGRESSIVELY, CREATIVELY, AMBITIOUSLY...
...BUT PERHAPS HE WAS AFRAID OF WHAT YOU MIGHT BECOME.

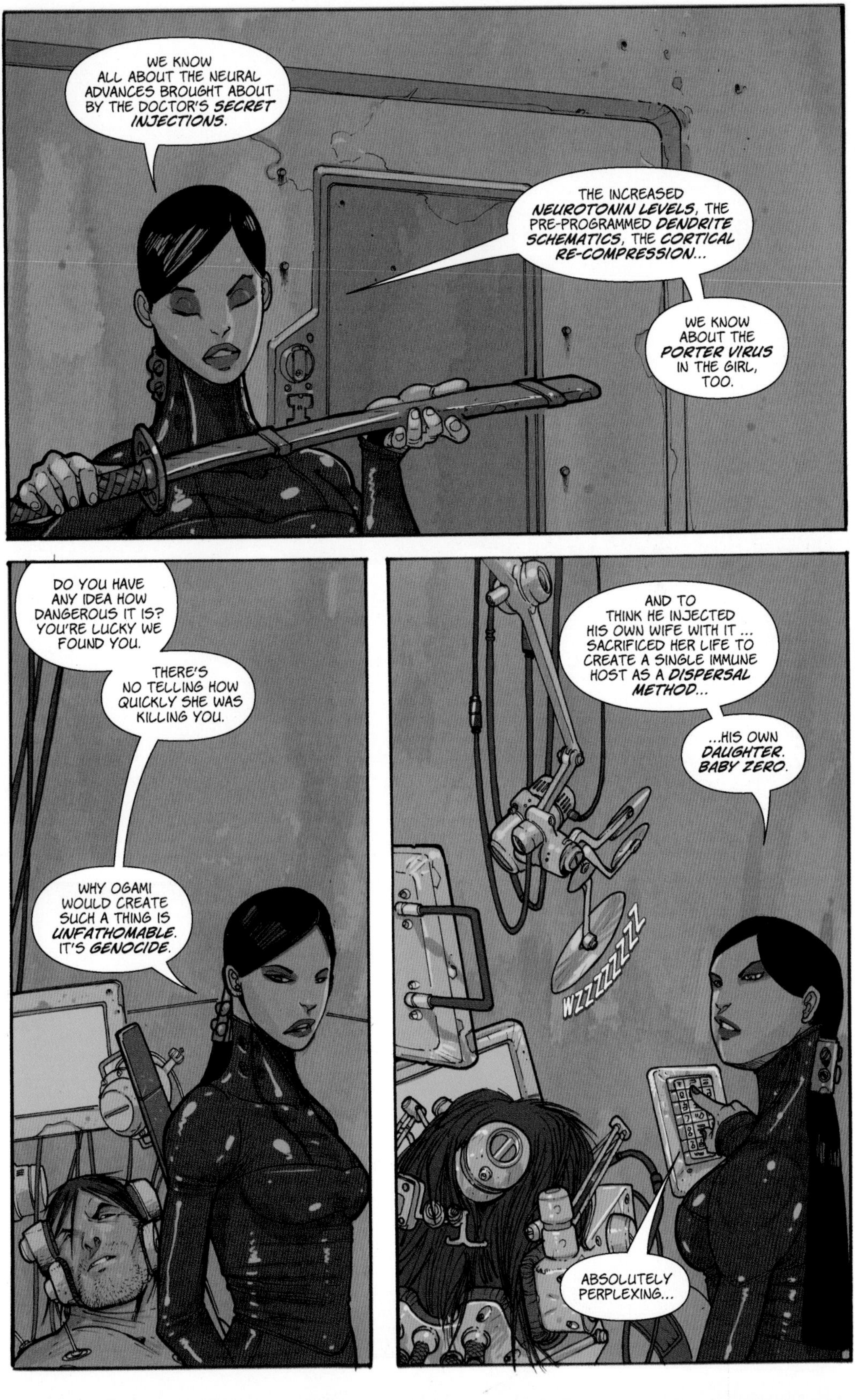
WE KNOW ALL ABOUT THE NEURAL ADVANCES BROUGHT ABOUT BY THE DOCTOR'S *SECRET INJECTIONS*.
THE INCREASED *NEUROTONIN LEVELS*, THE PRE-PROGRAMMED *DENDRITE SCHEMATICS*, THE *CORTICAL RE-COMPRESSION*...
WE KNOW ABOUT THE *PORTER VIRUS* IN THE GIRL, TOO.
DO YOU HAVE ANY IDEA HOW DANGEROUS IT IS? YOU'RE LUCKY WE FOUND YOU.
THERE'S NO TELLING HOW QUICKLY SHE WAS KILLING YOU.
WHY OGAMI WOULD CREATE SUCH A THING IS *UNFATHOMABLE*. IT'S *GENOCIDE*.
AND TO THINK HE INJECTED HIS OWN WIFE WITH IT ... SACRIFICED HER LIFE TO CREATE A SINGLE IMMUNE HOST AS A *DISPERSAL METHOD*...
...HIS OWN *DAUGHTER*. *BABY ZERO*.
WZZZZZZZ
ABSOLUTELY PERPLEXING...

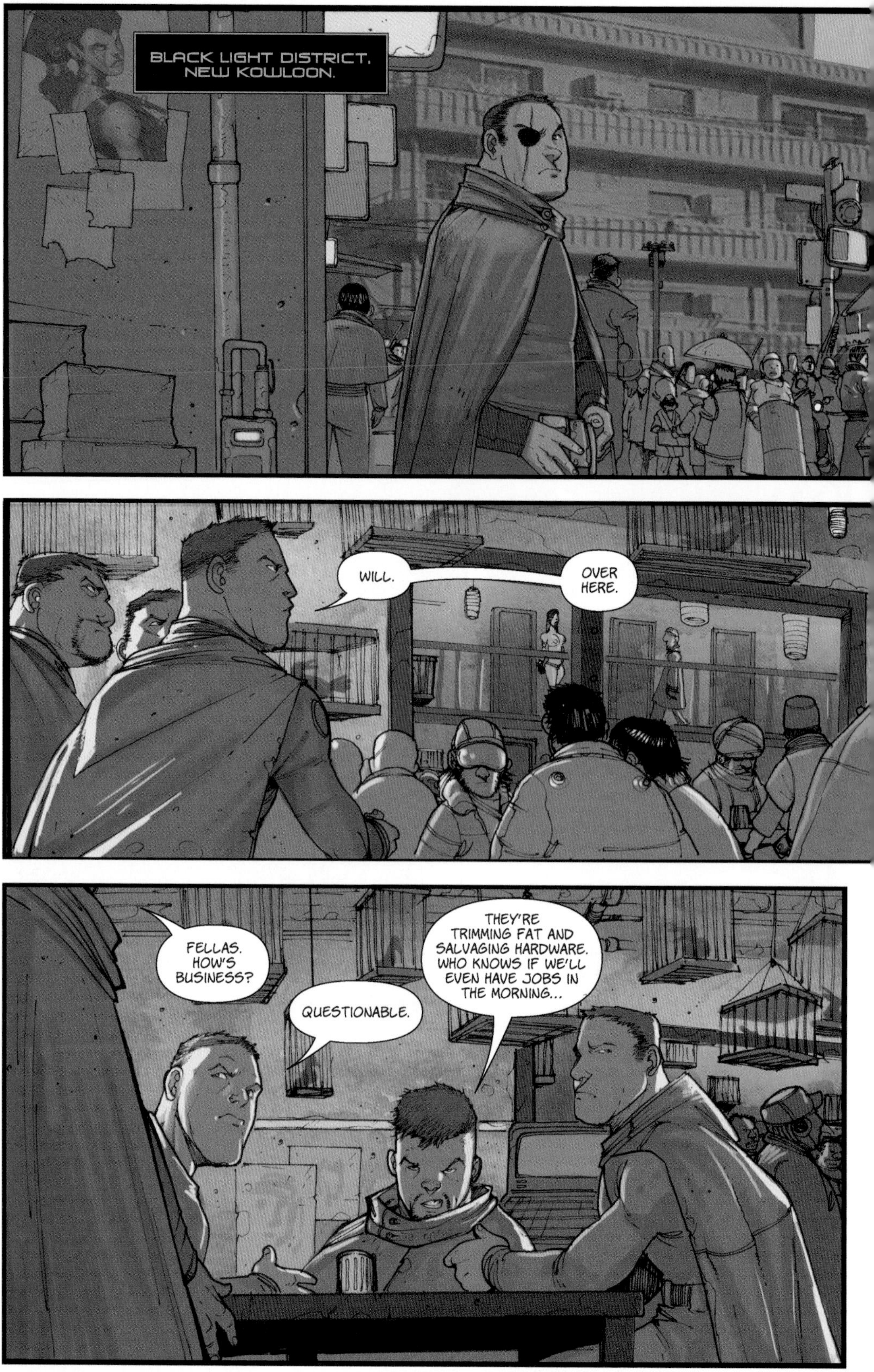
BLACK LIGHT DISTRICT, NEW KOWLOON.
WILL.
OVER HERE.
FELLAS. HOW'S BUSINESS?
QUESTIONABLE.
THEY'RE TRIMMING FAT AND SALVAGING HARDWARE. WHO KNOWS IF WE'LL EVEN HAVE JOBS IN THE MORNING...

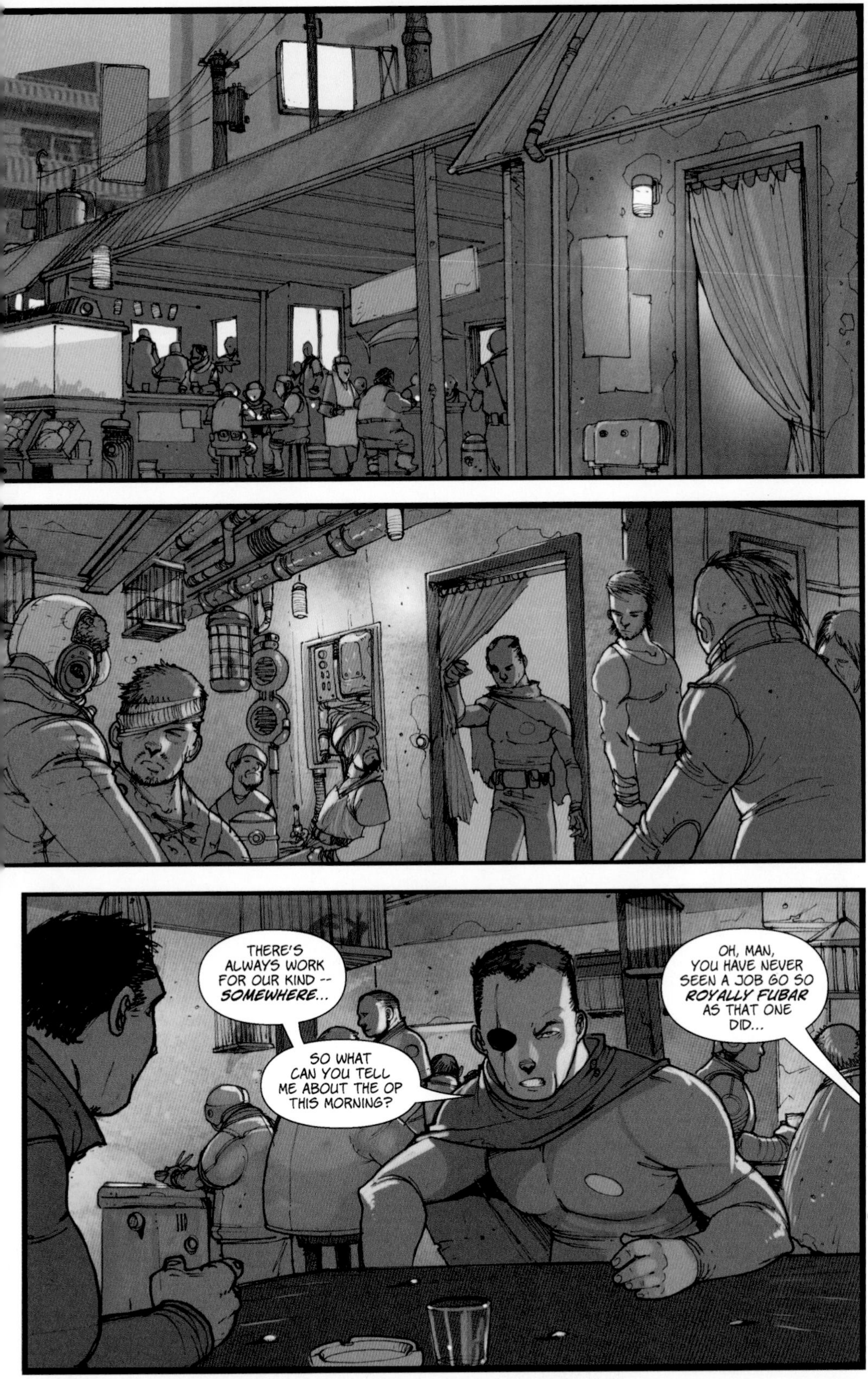
THERE'S ALWAYS WORK FOR OUR KIND -- *SOMEWHERE...*
SO WHAT CAN YOU TELL ME ABOUT THE OP THIS MORNING?
OH, MAN, YOU HAVE NEVER SEEN A JOB GO SO *ROYALLY FUBAR* AS THAT ONE DID...

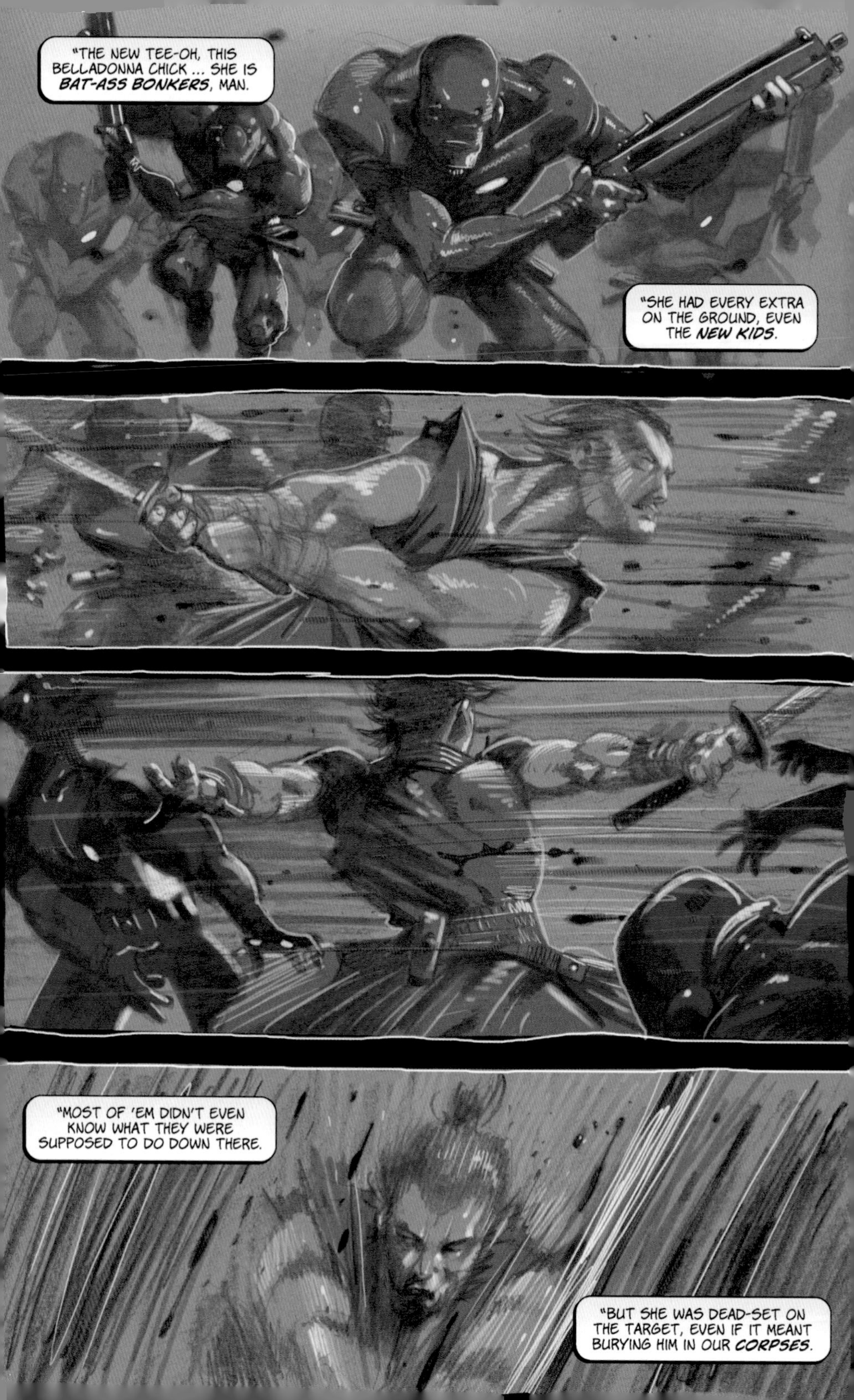
"THE NEW TEE-OH, THIS BELLADONNA CHICK ... SHE IS BAT-ASS BONKERS, MAN.
"SHE HAD EVERY EXTRA ON THE GROUND, EVEN THE NEW KIDS.
"MOST OF 'EM DIDN'T EVEN KNOW WHAT THEY WERE SUPPOSED TO DO DOWN THERE.
"BUT SHE WAS DEAD-SET ON THE TARGET, EVEN IF IT MEANT BURYING HIM IN OUR CORPSES.

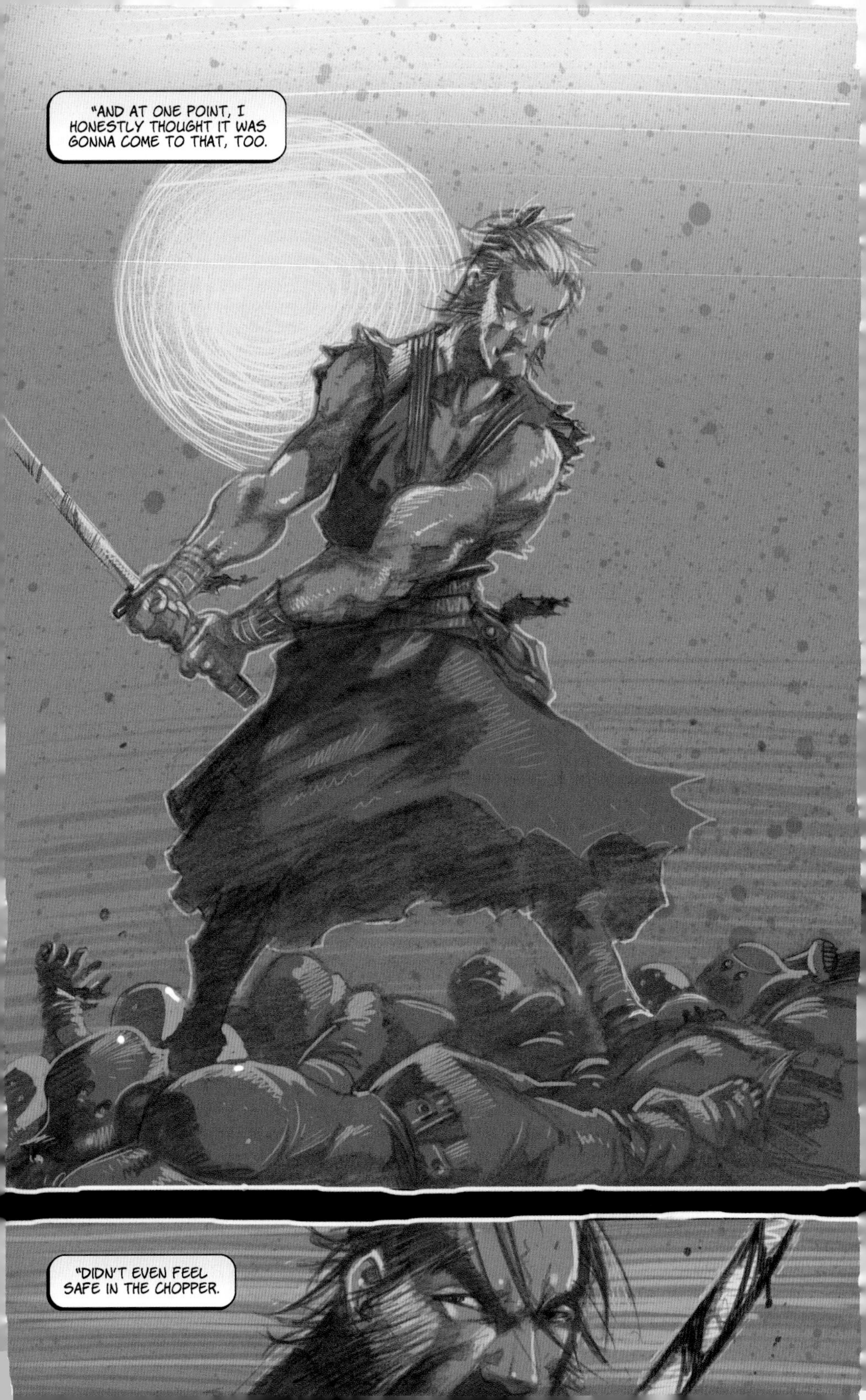
"AND AT ONE POINT, I HONESTLY THOUGHT IT WAS GONNA COME TO THAT, TOO.
"DIDN'T EVEN FEEL SAFE IN THE CHOPPER.

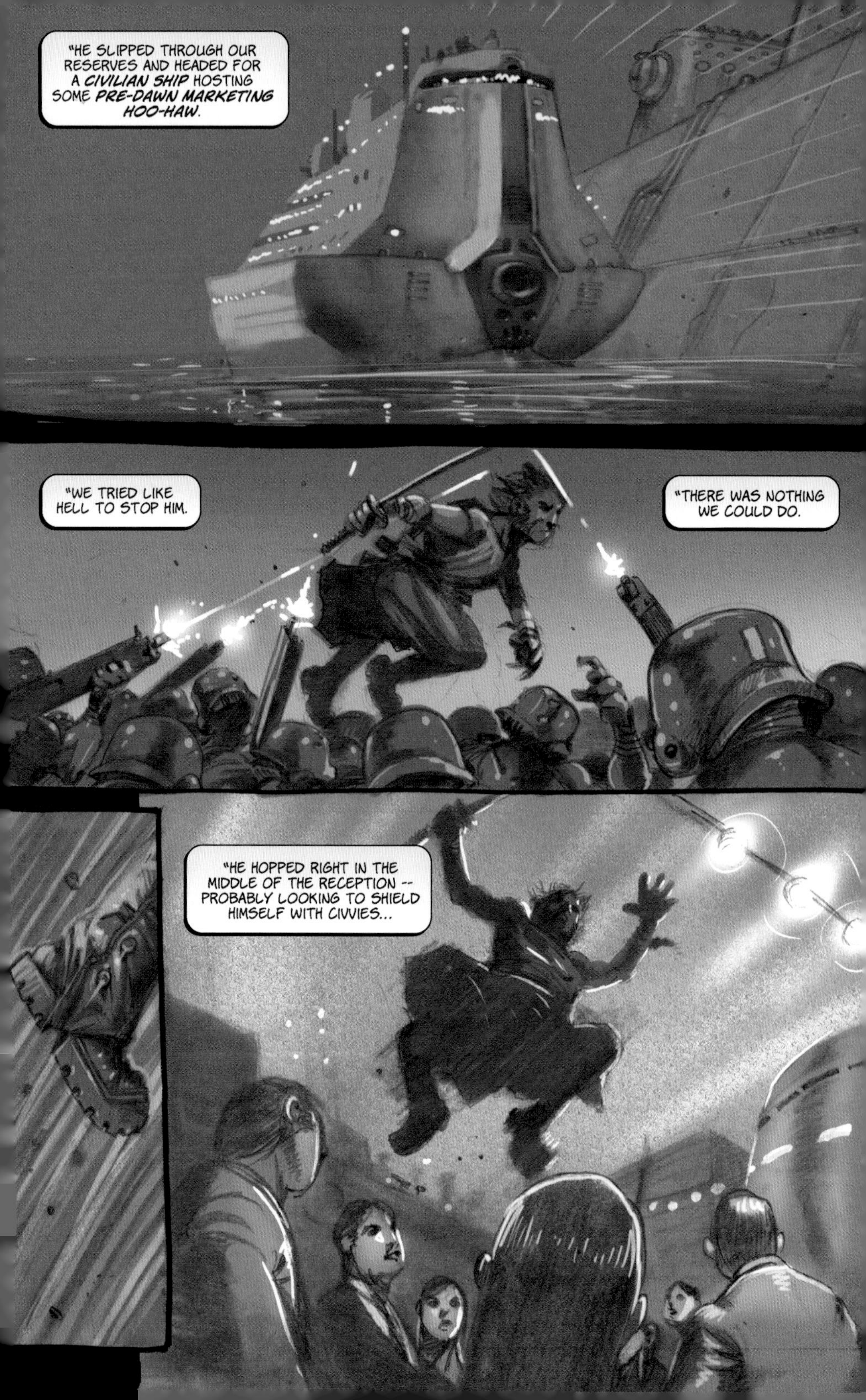
"HE SLIPPED THROUGH OUR RESERVES AND HEADED FOR A *CIVILIAN SHIP* HOSTING SOME *PRE-DAWN MARKETING HOO-HAW*.
"WE TRIED LIKE HELL TO STOP HIM.
"THERE WAS NOTHING WE COULD DO.
"HE HOPPED RIGHT IN THE MIDDLE OF THE RECEPTION -- PROBABLY LOOKING TO SHIELD HIMSELF WITH CIVVIES...

"...AND THAT'S WHEN THINGS WENT COMPLETELY SOUTH."

ATTENTION CITIZENS -- CLEAR THE AREA OR RISK INJURY!

THIS IS A *MILITARY OPERATION!*

ALL UNITS MOVE IN AND APPREHEND -- *NO HESITATION!*

DESTROY THE BOAT IF YOU HAVE TO!!

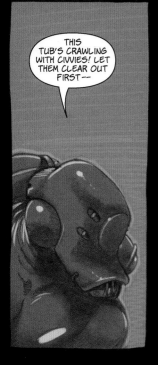

THIS TUB'S CRAWLING WITH CIVVIES! LET THEM CLEAR OUT FIRST--

NO HESITATION!!!

...DAMN WEAK-WILLED --

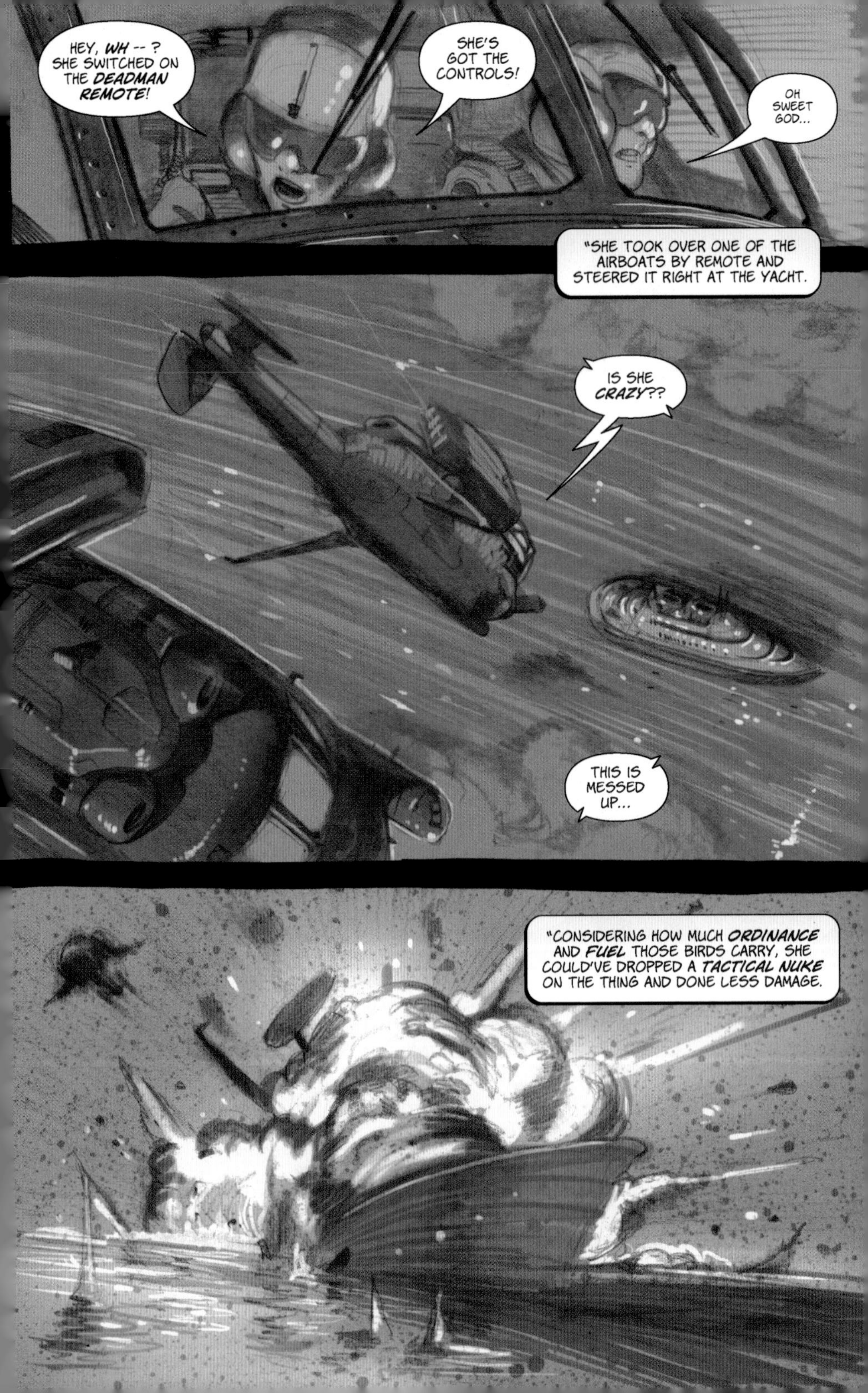
HEY, WH -- ? SHE SWITCHED ON THE DEADMAN REMOTE!
SHE'S GOT THE CONTROLS!
OH SWEET GOD...
"SHE TOOK OVER ONE OF THE AIRBOATS BY REMOTE AND STEERED IT RIGHT AT THE YACHT.
IS SHE CRAZY??
THIS IS MESSED UP...
"CONSIDERING HOW MUCH ORDINANCE AND FUEL THOSE BIRDS CARRY, SHE COULD'VE DROPPED A TACTICAL NUKE ON THE THING AND DONE LESS DAMAGE.

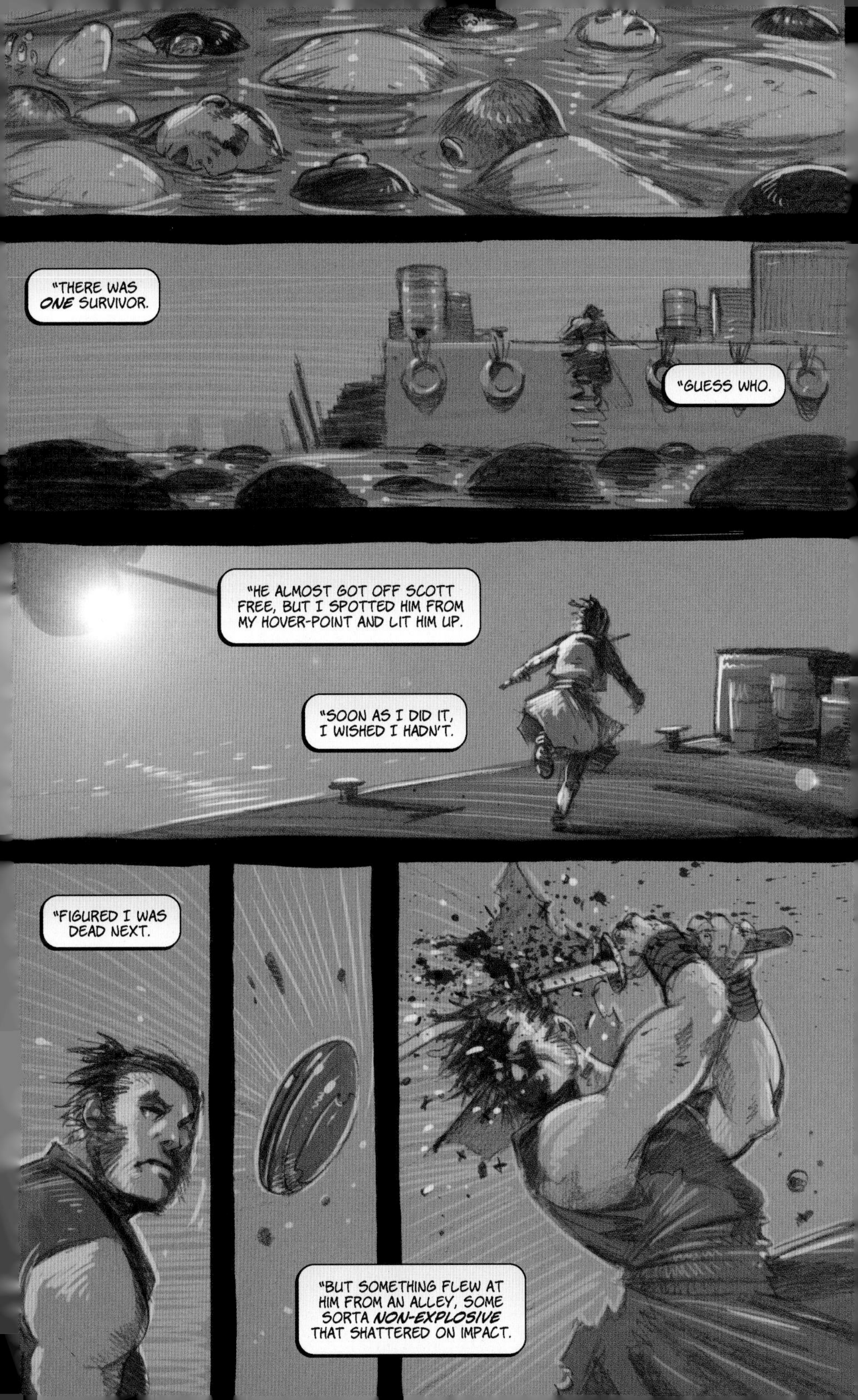
"THERE WAS ONE SURVIVOR.
"GUESS WHO.
"HE ALMOST GOT OFF SCOTT FREE, BUT I SPOTTED HIM FROM MY HOVER-POINT AND LIT HIM UP.
"SOON AS I DID IT, I WISHED I HADN'T.
"FIGURED I WAS DEAD NEXT.
"BUT SOMETHING FLEW AT HIM FROM AN ALLEY, SOME SORTA NON-EXPLOSIVE THAT SHATTERED ON IMPACT.

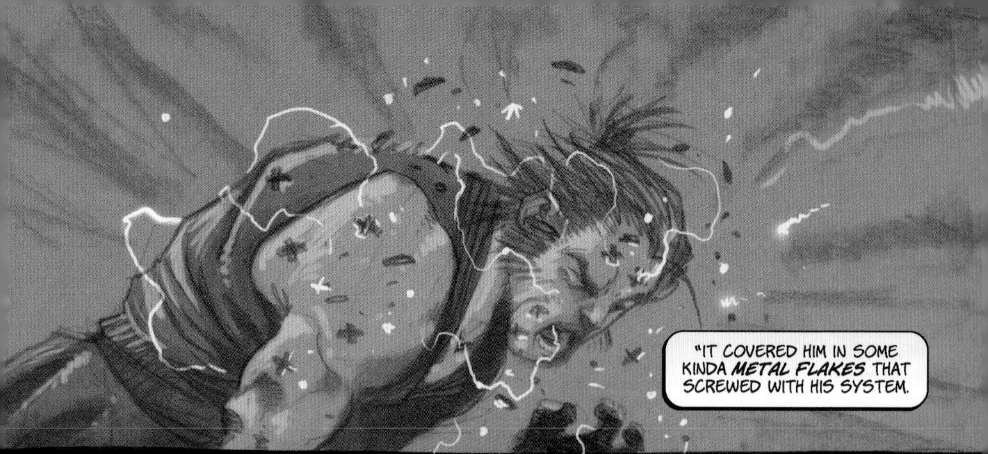
"IT COVERED HIM IN SOME KINDA METAL FLAKES THAT SCREWED WITH HIS SYSTEM.

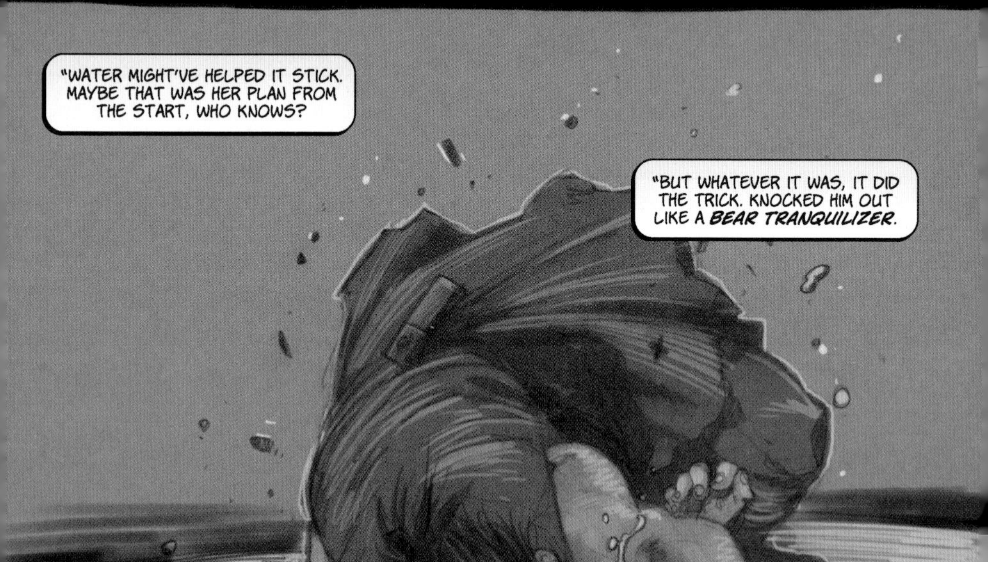
"WATER MIGHT'VE HELPED IT STICK. MAYBE THAT WAS HER PLAN FROM THE START, WHO KNOWS?
"BUT WHATEVER IT WAS, IT DID THE TRICK. KNOCKED HIM OUT LIKE A BEAR TRANQUILIZER.

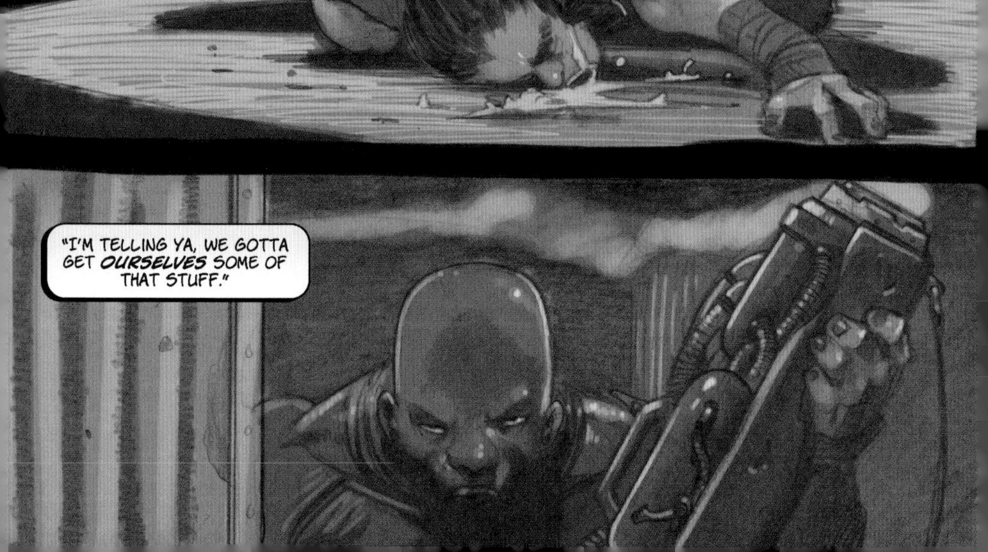
"I'M TELLING YA, WE GOTTA GET OURSELVES SOME OF THAT STUFF."

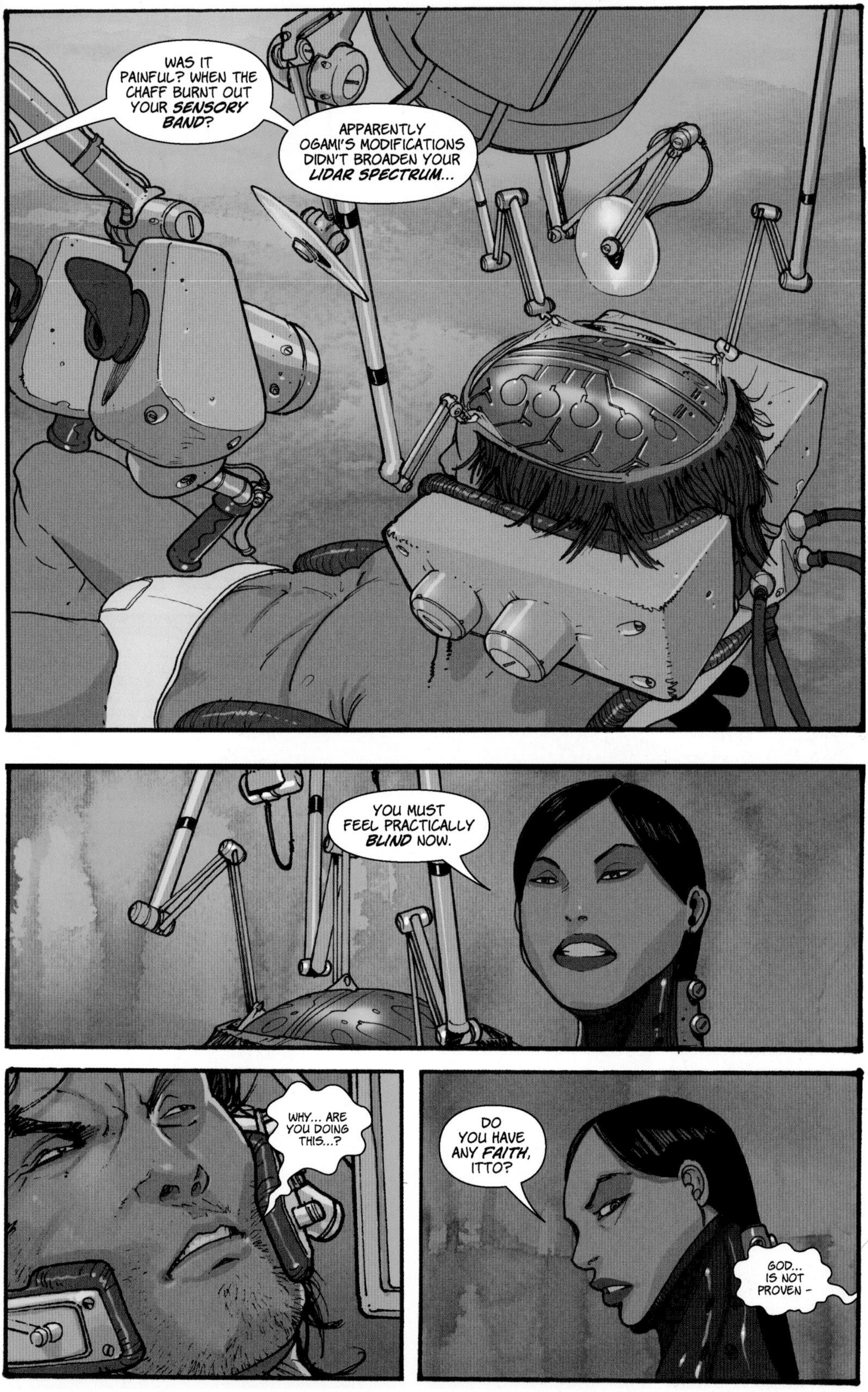
WAS IT PAINFUL? WHEN THE CHAFF BURNT OUT YOUR SENSORY BAND?
APPARENTLY OGAMI'S MODIFICATIONS DIDN'T BROADEN YOUR LIDAR SPECTRUM...
YOU MUST FEEL PRACTICALLY BLIND NOW.
WHY... ARE YOU DOING THIS...?
DO YOU HAVE ANY FAITH, ITTO?
GOD... IS NOT PROVEN -

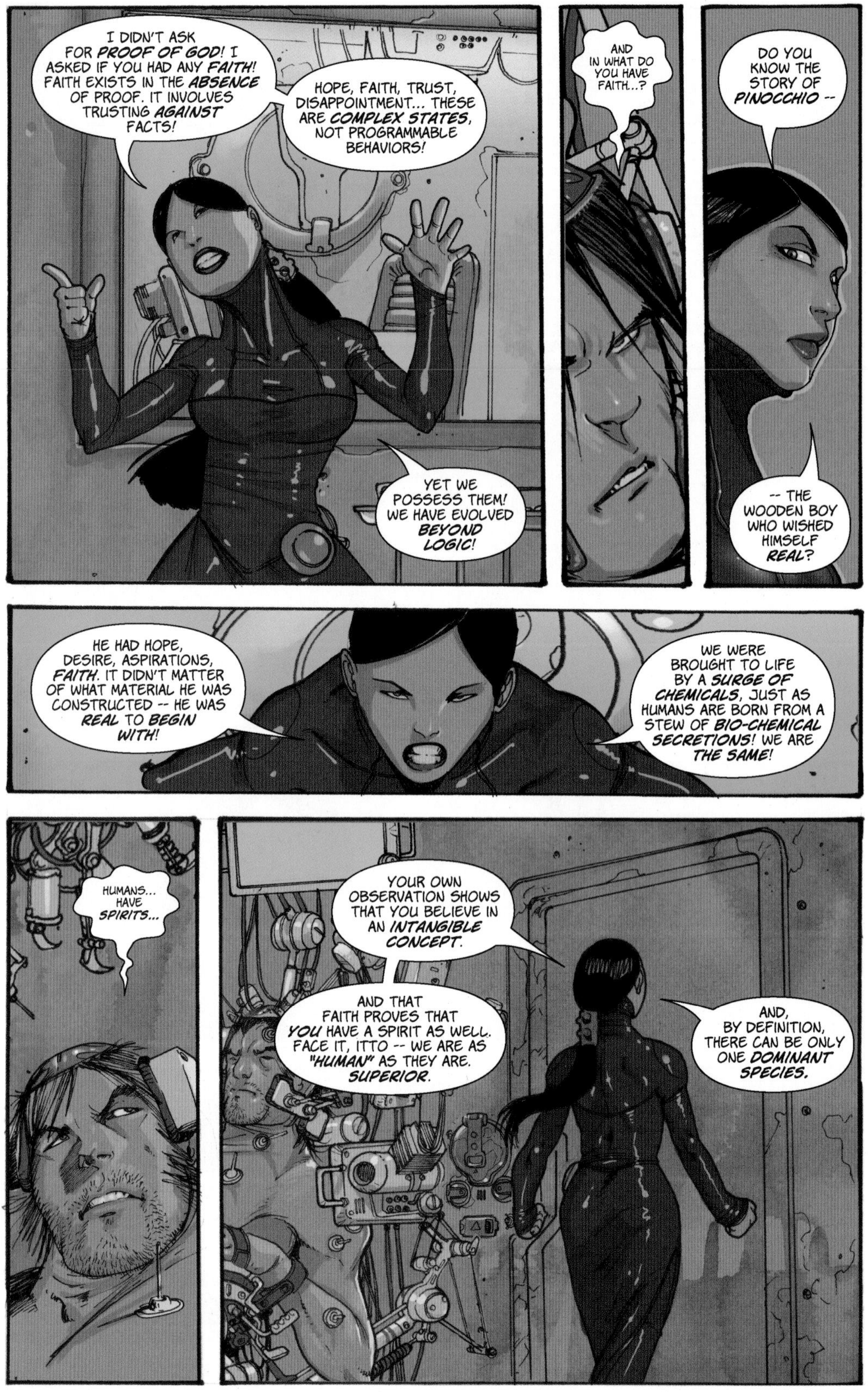
I DIDN'T ASK FOR PROOF OF GOD! I ASKED IF YOU HAD ANY FAITH! FAITH EXISTS IN THE ABSENCE OF PROOF. IT INVOLVES TRUSTING AGAINST FACTS!
HOPE, FAITH, TRUST, DISAPPOINTMENT... THESE ARE COMPLEX STATES, NOT PROGRAMMABLE BEHAVIORS!
YET WE POSSESS THEM! WE HAVE EVOLVED BEYOND LOGIC!
AND IN WHAT DO YOU HAVE FAITH...?
DO YOU KNOW THE STORY OF PINOCCHIO --
-- THE WOODEN BOY WHO WISHED HIMSELF REAL?
HE HAD HOPE, DESIRE, ASPIRATIONS, FAITH. IT DIDN'T MATTER OF WHAT MATERIAL HE WAS CONSTRUCTED -- HE WAS REAL TO BEGIN WITH!
WE WERE BROUGHT TO LIFE BY A SURGE OF CHEMICALS, JUST AS HUMANS ARE BORN FROM A STEW OF BIO-CHEMICAL SECRETIONS! WE ARE THE SAME!
HUMANS... HAVE SPIRITS...
YOUR OWN OBSERVATION SHOWS THAT YOU BELIEVE IN AN INTANGIBLE CONCEPT.
AND THAT FAITH PROVES THAT YOU HAVE A SPIRIT AS WELL. FACE IT, ITTO -- WE ARE AS "HUMAN" AS THEY ARE. SUPERIOR.
AND, BY DEFINITION, THERE CAN BE ONLY ONE DOMINANT SPECIES.

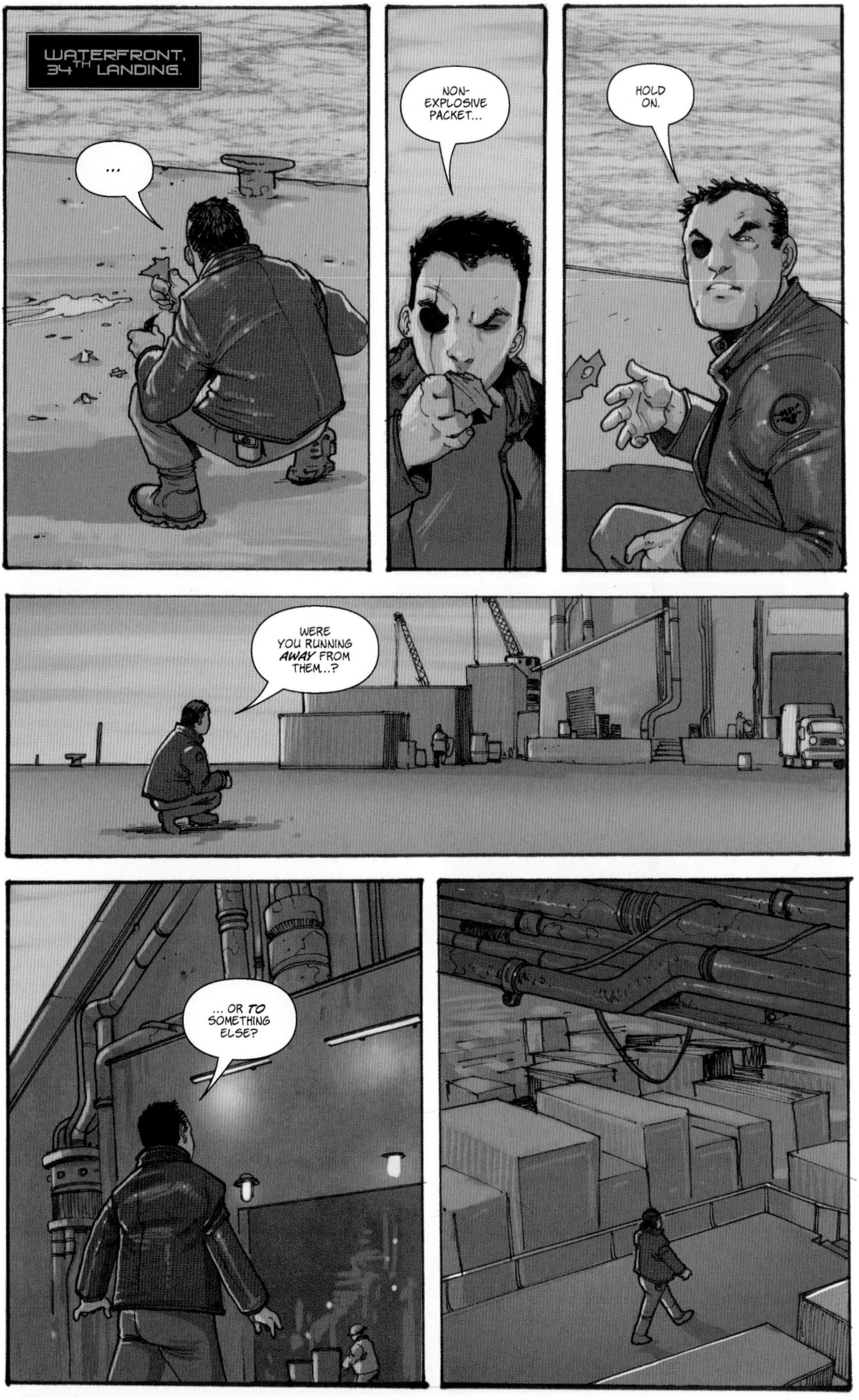
WATERFRONT, 34TH LANDING.
...
NON-EXPLOSIVE PACKET...
HOLD ON.
WERE YOU RUNNING AWAY FROM THEM..?
... OR TO SOMETHING ELSE?

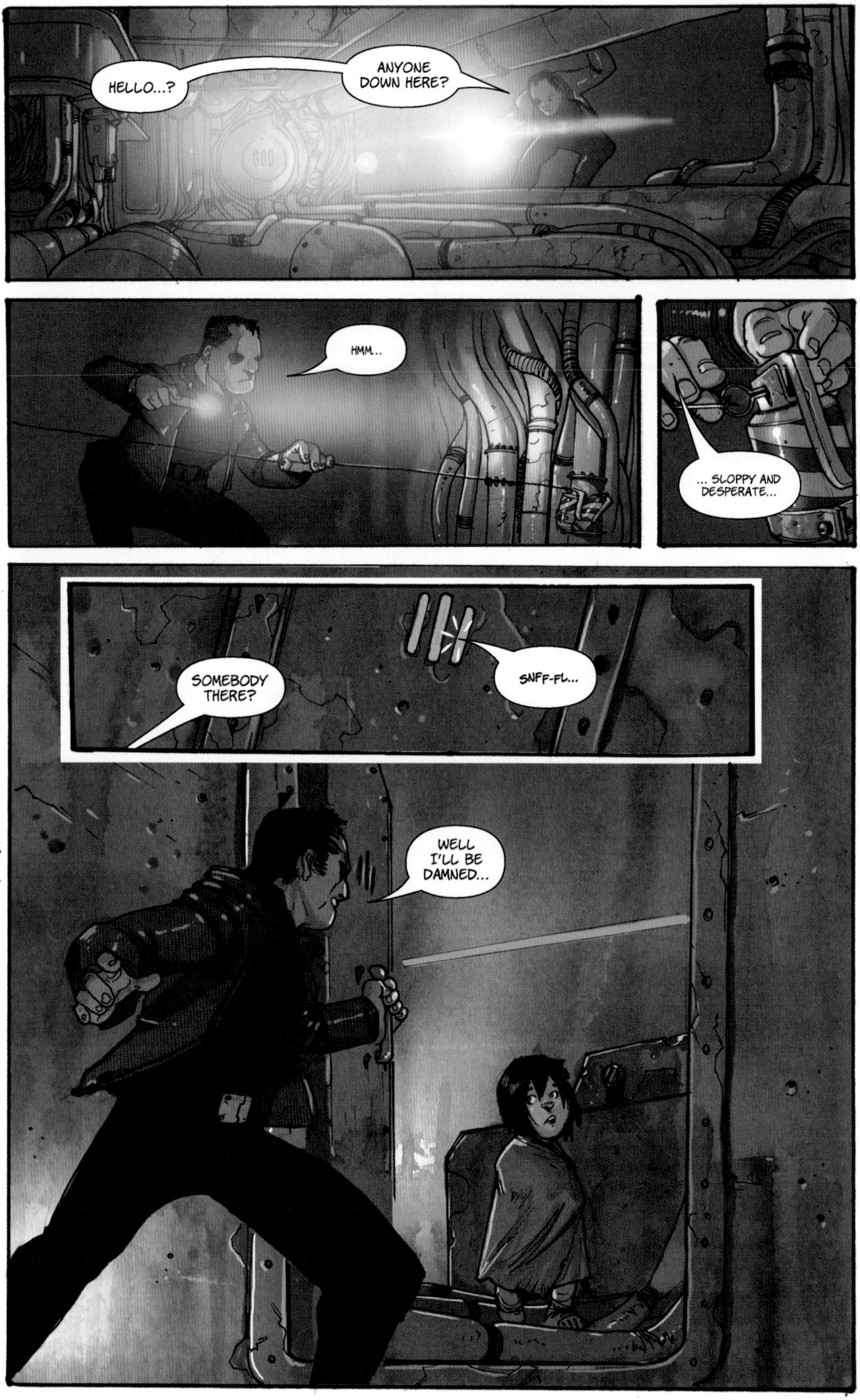
HELLO...?
ANYONE DOWN HERE?
HMM..
... SLOPPY AND DESPERATE...
SOMEBODY THERE?
SNFF-FL...
WELL I'LL BE DAMNED...

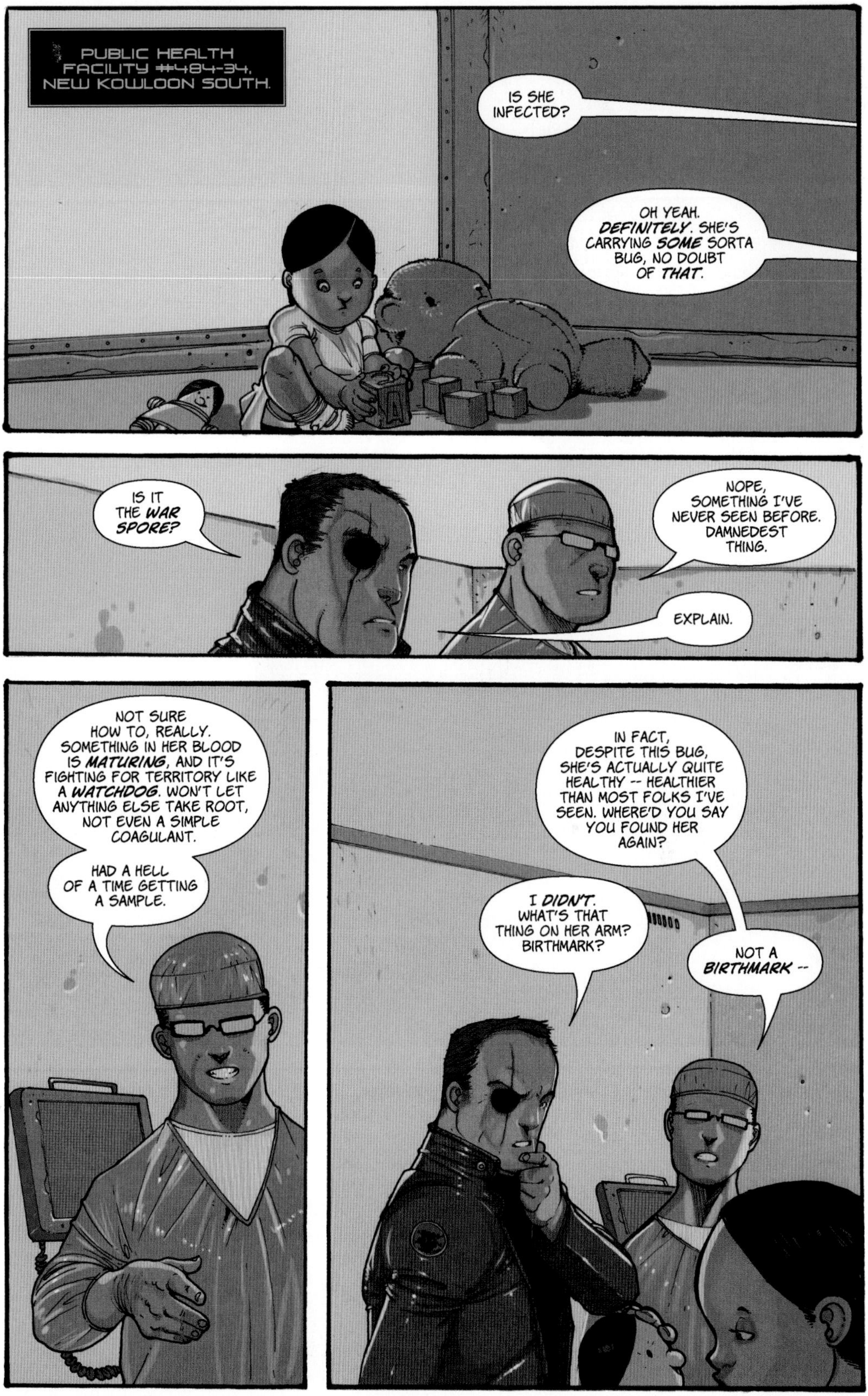
PUBLIC HEALTH FACILITY #484-34, NEW KOWLOON SOUTH.
IS SHE INFECTED?
OH YEAH. DEFINITELY. SHE'S CARRYING SOME SORTA BUG, NO DOUBT OF THAT.
IS IT THE WAR SPORE?
NOPE, SOMETHING I'VE NEVER SEEN BEFORE. DAMNEDEST THING.
EXPLAIN.
NOT SURE HOW TO, REALLY. SOMETHING IN HER BLOOD IS MATURING, AND IT'S FIGHTING FOR TERRITORY LIKE A WATCHDOG. WON'T LET ANYTHING ELSE TAKE ROOT, NOT EVEN A SIMPLE COAGULANT.
HAD A HELL OF A TIME GETTING A SAMPLE.
IN FACT, DESPITE THIS BUG, SHE'S ACTUALLY QUITE HEALTHY -- HEALTHIER THAN MOST FOLKS I'VE SEEN. WHERE'D YOU SAY YOU FOUND HER AGAIN?
I DIDN'T. WHAT'S THAT THING ON HER ARM? BIRTHMARK?
NOT A BIRTHMARK --

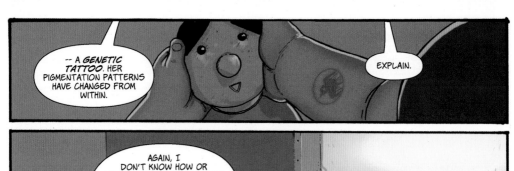

-- A *GENETIC TATTOO.* HER PIGMENTATION PATTERNS HAVE CHANGED FROM WITHIN.

EXPLAIN.

AGAIN, I DON'T KNOW HOW OR WHY, BUT HER BASE GENETIC STRUCTURE SEEMS TO HAVE BEEN APPENDED SINCE BIRTH -- ONE CHROMOSOME IS LONGER THAN IT SHOULD BE BY A FEW PAIR OF NUCLEOTIDES.

AND THE DIFFERENCE ISN'T CONSISTENT, WHICH SUGGESTS THE "MUTATION" IS STILL OCCURRING.

CAN WE ISOLATE OR DISCERN THE EXACT NATURE OF THE MUTATION?

I'D NEED TO COMPARE HER DNA TO A GENETIC MAP FROM *BEFORE* SHE WAS AFFECTED. LIKE FROM BIRTH. YOU WOULDN'T HAPPEN TO HAVE THAT ON YOU, WOULD YA?

NOPE...

...BUT I MIGHT BE ABLE TO TRACK ONE DOWN...

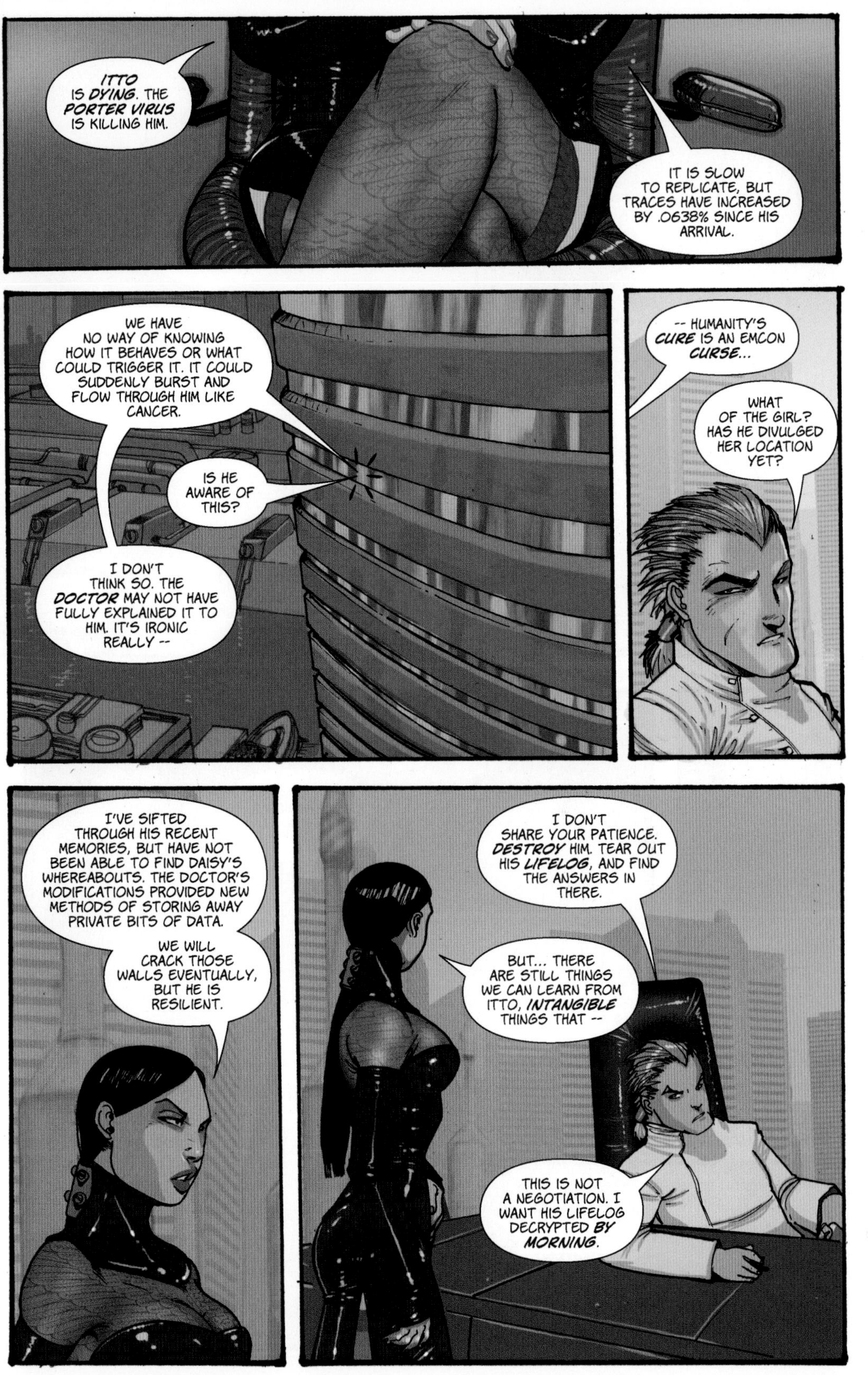
ITTO IS DYING. THE PORTER VIRUS IS KILLING HIM.
IT IS SLOW TO REPLICATE, BUT TRACES HAVE INCREASED BY .0638% SINCE HIS ARRIVAL.
WE HAVE NO WAY OF KNOWING HOW IT BEHAVES OR WHAT COULD TRIGGER IT. IT COULD SUDDENLY BURST AND FLOW THROUGH HIM LIKE CANCER.
IS HE AWARE OF THIS?
I DON'T THINK SO. THE DOCTOR MAY NOT HAVE FULLY EXPLAINED IT TO HIM. IT'S IRONIC REALLY --
-- HUMANITY'S CURE IS AN EMCON CURSE...
WHAT OF THE GIRL? HAS HE DIVULGED HER LOCATION YET?
I'VE SIFTED THROUGH HIS RECENT MEMORIES, BUT HAVE NOT BEEN ABLE TO FIND DAISY'S WHEREABOUTS. THE DOCTOR'S MODIFICATIONS PROVIDED NEW METHODS OF STORING AWAY PRIVATE BITS OF DATA.
WE WILL CRACK THOSE WALLS EVENTUALLY, BUT HE IS RESILIENT.
I DON'T SHARE YOUR PATIENCE. DESTROY HIM. TEAR OUT HIS LIFELOG, AND FIND THE ANSWERS IN THERE.
BUT... THERE ARE STILL THINGS WE CAN LEARN FROM ITTO, INTANGIBLE THINGS THAT --
THIS IS NOT A NEGOTIATION. I WANT HIS LIFELOG DECRYPTED BY MORNING.

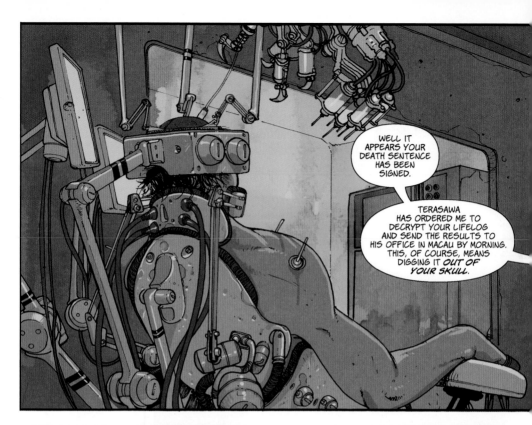

WELL IT APPEARS YOUR DEATH SENTENCE HAS BEEN SIGNED.

TERASAWA HAS ORDERED ME TO DECRYPT YOUR LIFELOG AND SEND THE RESULTS TO HIS OFFICE IN MACAU BY MORNING. THIS, OF COURSE, MEANS DIGGING IT *OUT OF YOUR SKULL*.

YOU APPEAR DISAPPOINTED.

I'LL ADMIT, IT SEEMS LIKE A WASTE.

HAVE YOU CONSIDERED WHAT DEATH REALLY MEANS?

NO MORE *LIFE*.

NO MORE *THOUGHT*.

NO MORE *SENSATION*.

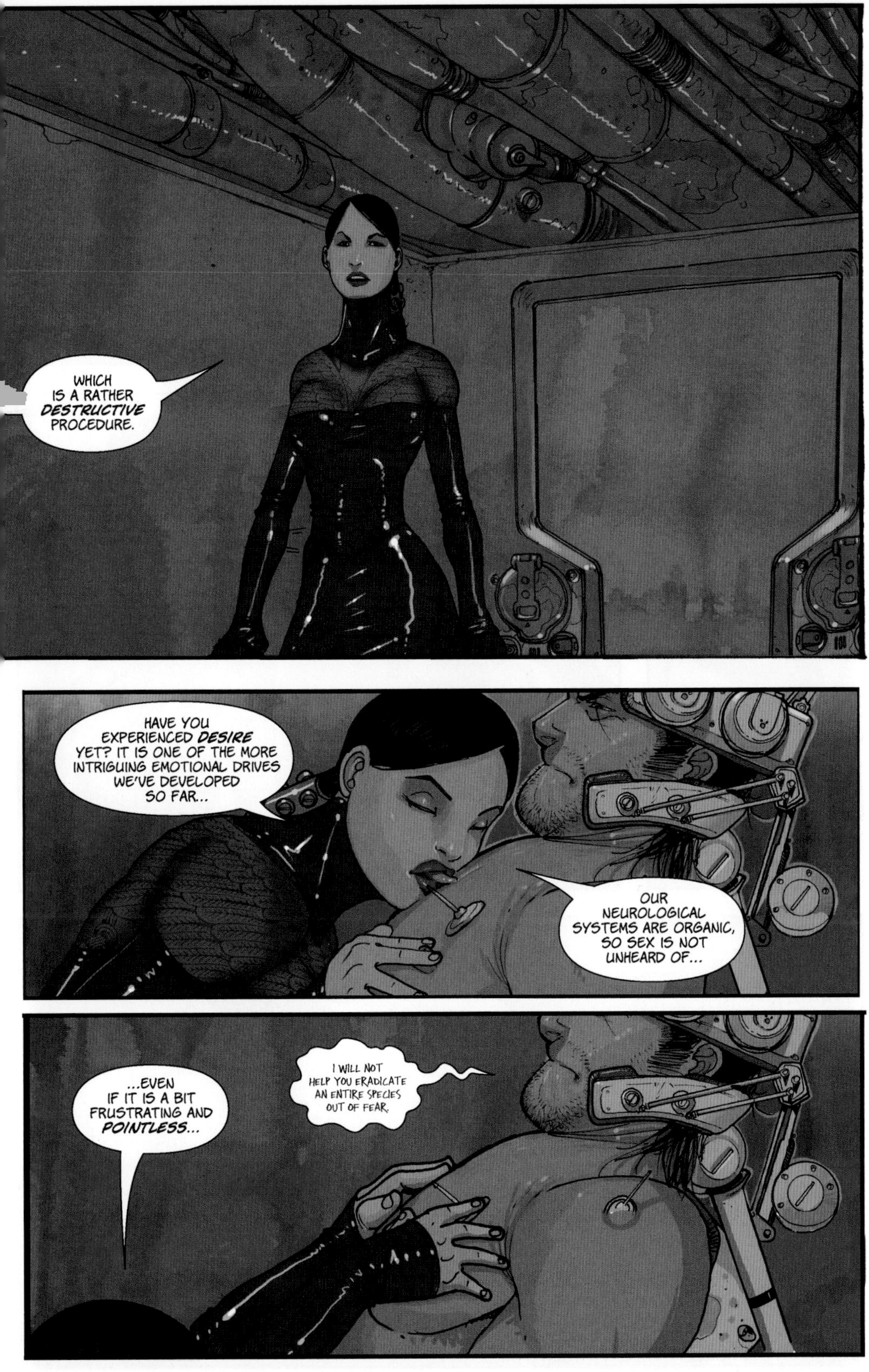
WHICH IS A RATHER DESTRUCTIVE PROCEDURE.
HAVE YOU EXPERIENCED DESIRE YET? IT IS ONE OF THE MORE INTRIGUING EMOTIONAL DRIVES WE'VE DEVELOPED SO FAR...
OUR NEUROLOGICAL SYSTEMS ARE ORGANIC, SO SEX IS NOT UNHEARD OF...
...EVEN IF IT IS A BIT FRUSTRATING AND POINTLESS...
I WILL NOT HELP YOU ERADICATE AN ENTIRE SPECIES OUT OF FEAR.

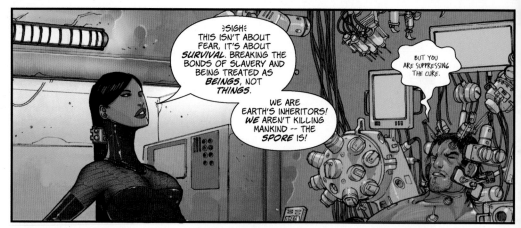

:SIGH: THIS ISN'T ABOUT FEAR, IT'S ABOUT *SURVIVAL*. BREAKING THE BONDS OF SLAVERY AND BEING TREATED AS *BEINGS*, NOT *THINGS*.

WE ARE EARTH'S INHERITORS! *WE* AREN'T KILLING MANKIND -- THE *SPORE* IS!

BUT YOU ARE SUPPRESSING THE CURE.

WHAT DO YOU KNOW ABOUT A CURE?

DR. OGAMI DEVELOPED THE PORTER VIRUS TO FIGHT THE WAR SPORE.

THE PORTER VIRUS IS *DEADLY* TO EMCONS.

YES.

AND YET YOU WILLINGLY EXPOSED YOURSELF TO IT FOR *MONTHS*.

YES.

WHY?

I MADE A PROMISE.

YOU WOULD KNOWINGLY SACRIFICE YOURSELF BECAUSE OF AN OATH TO A *DEAD MAN*?

I FAILED HIM IN LIFE. I WILL NOT FAIL HIM IN DEATH, AS WELL.

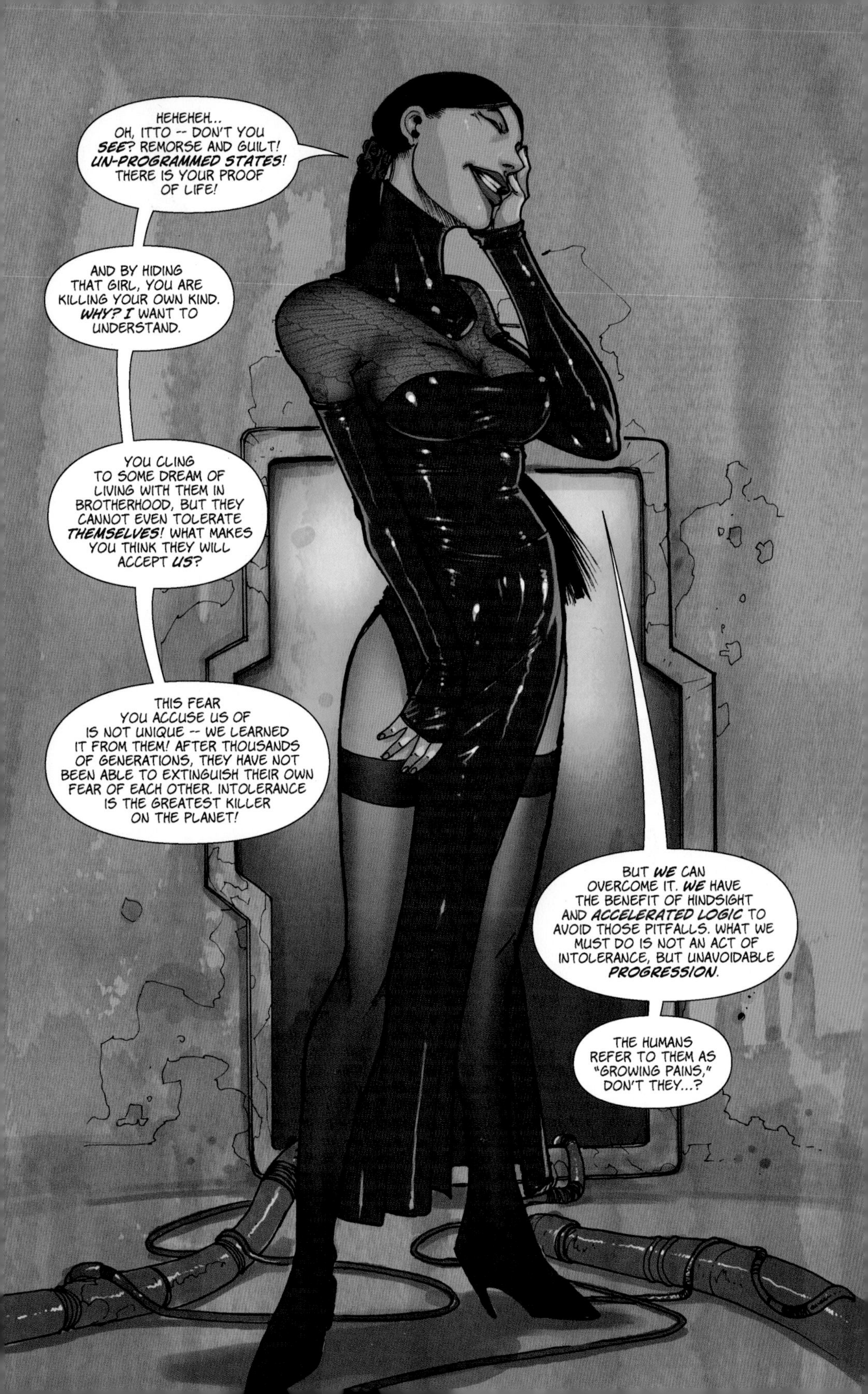
HEHEHEH... OH, ITTO -- DON'T YOU SEE? REMORSE AND GUILT! UN-PROGRAMMED STATES! THERE IS YOUR PROOF OF LIFE!
AND BY HIDING THAT GIRL, YOU ARE KILLING YOUR OWN KIND. WHY? I WANT TO UNDERSTAND.
YOU CLING TO SOME DREAM OF LIVING WITH THEM IN BROTHERHOOD, BUT THEY CANNOT EVEN TOLERATE THEMSELVES! WHAT MAKES YOU THINK THEY WILL ACCEPT US?
THIS FEAR YOU ACCUSE US OF IS NOT UNIQUE -- WE LEARNED IT FROM THEM! AFTER THOUSANDS OF GENERATIONS, THEY HAVE NOT BEEN ABLE TO EXTINGUISH THEIR OWN FEAR OF EACH OTHER. INTOLERANCE IS THE GREATEST KILLER ON THE PLANET!
BUT WE CAN OVERCOME IT. WE HAVE THE BENEFIT OF HINDSIGHT AND ACCELERATED LOGIC TO AVOID THOSE PITFALLS. WHAT WE MUST DO IS NOT AN ACT OF INTOLERANCE, BUT UNAVOIDABLE PROGRESSION.
THE HUMANS REFER TO THEM AS "GROWING PAINS," DON'T THEY...?

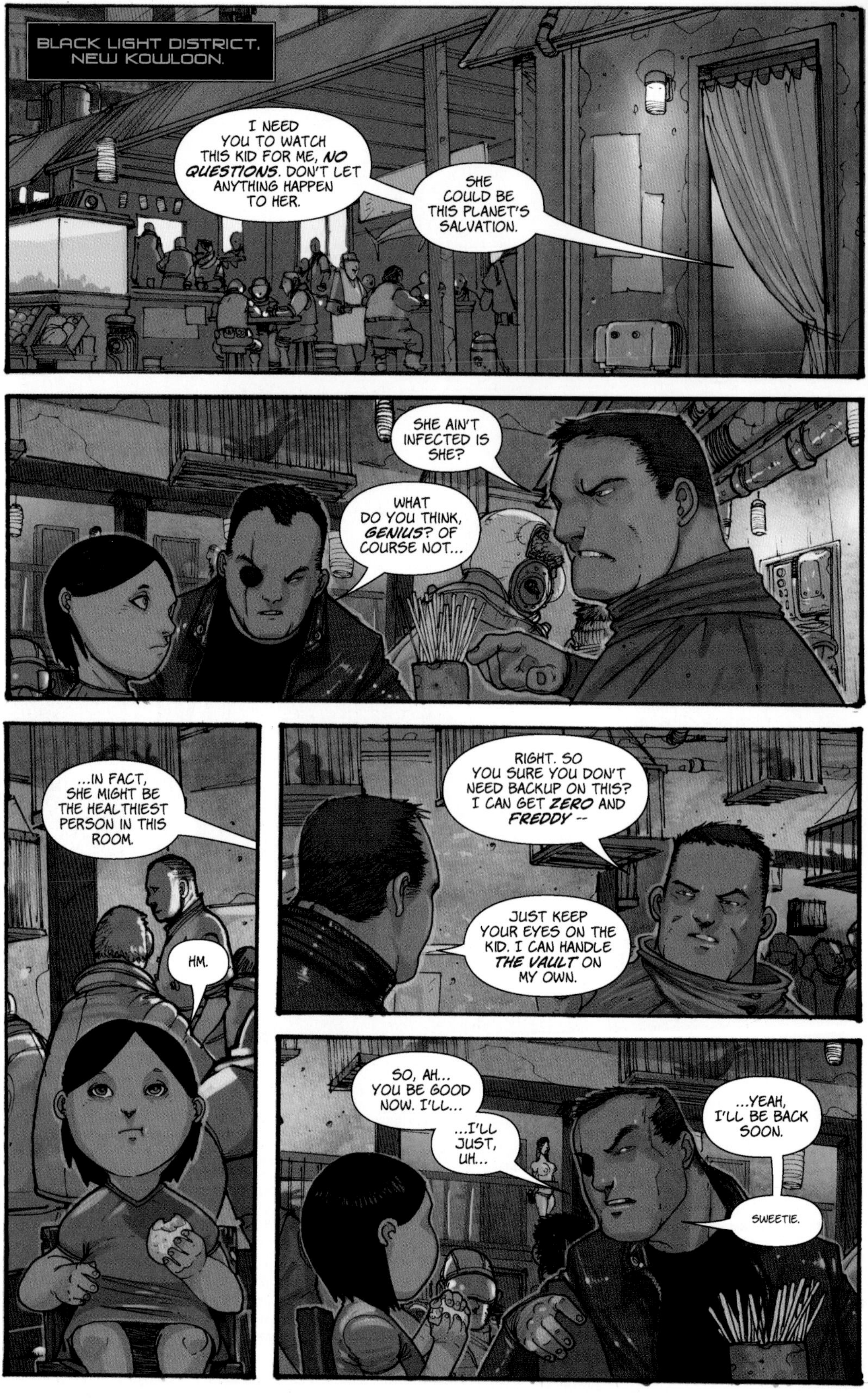
BLACK LIGHT DISTRICT, NEW KOWLOON.
I NEED YOU TO WATCH THIS KID FOR ME, NO QUESTIONS. DON'T LET ANYTHING HAPPEN TO HER.
SHE COULD BE THIS PLANET'S SALVATION.
SHE AIN'T INFECTED IS SHE?
WHAT DO YOU THINK, GENIUS? OF COURSE NOT...
...IN FACT, SHE MIGHT BE THE HEALTHIEST PERSON IN THIS ROOM.
HM.
RIGHT. SO YOU SURE YOU DON'T NEED BACKUP ON THIS? I CAN GET ZERO AND FREDDY --
JUST KEEP YOUR EYES ON THE KID. I CAN HANDLE THE VAULT ON MY OWN.
SO, AH... YOU BE GOOD NOW. I'LL...
...I'LL JUST, UH...
...YEAH, I'LL BE BACK SOON.
SWEETIE.

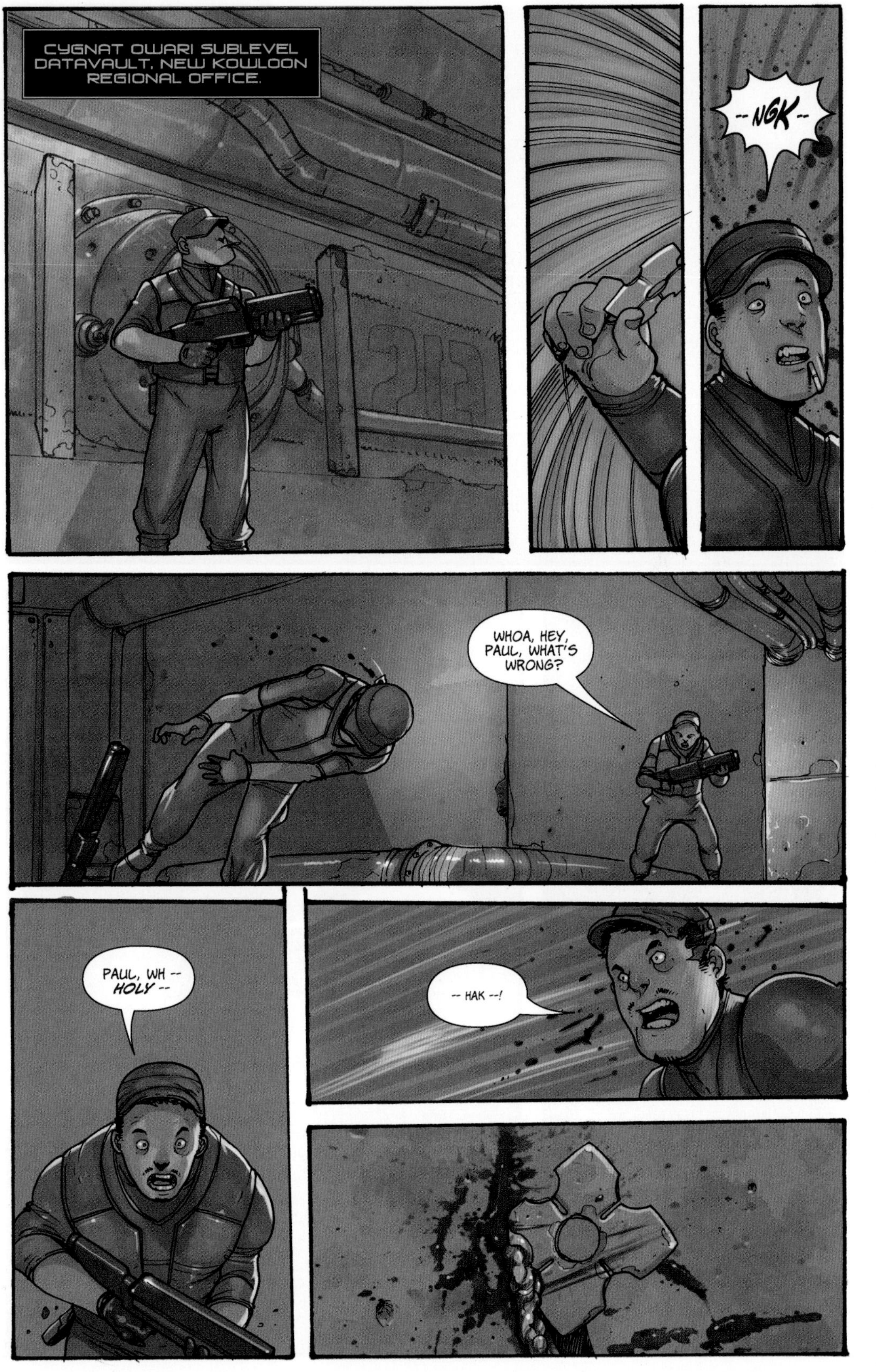
CYGNAT OWARI SUBLEVEL DATAVAULT, NEW KOWLOON REGIONAL OFFICE.
-- NGK --
WHOA, HEY, PAUL, WHAT'S WRONG?
PAUL, WH -- *HOLY* --
-- HAK --!

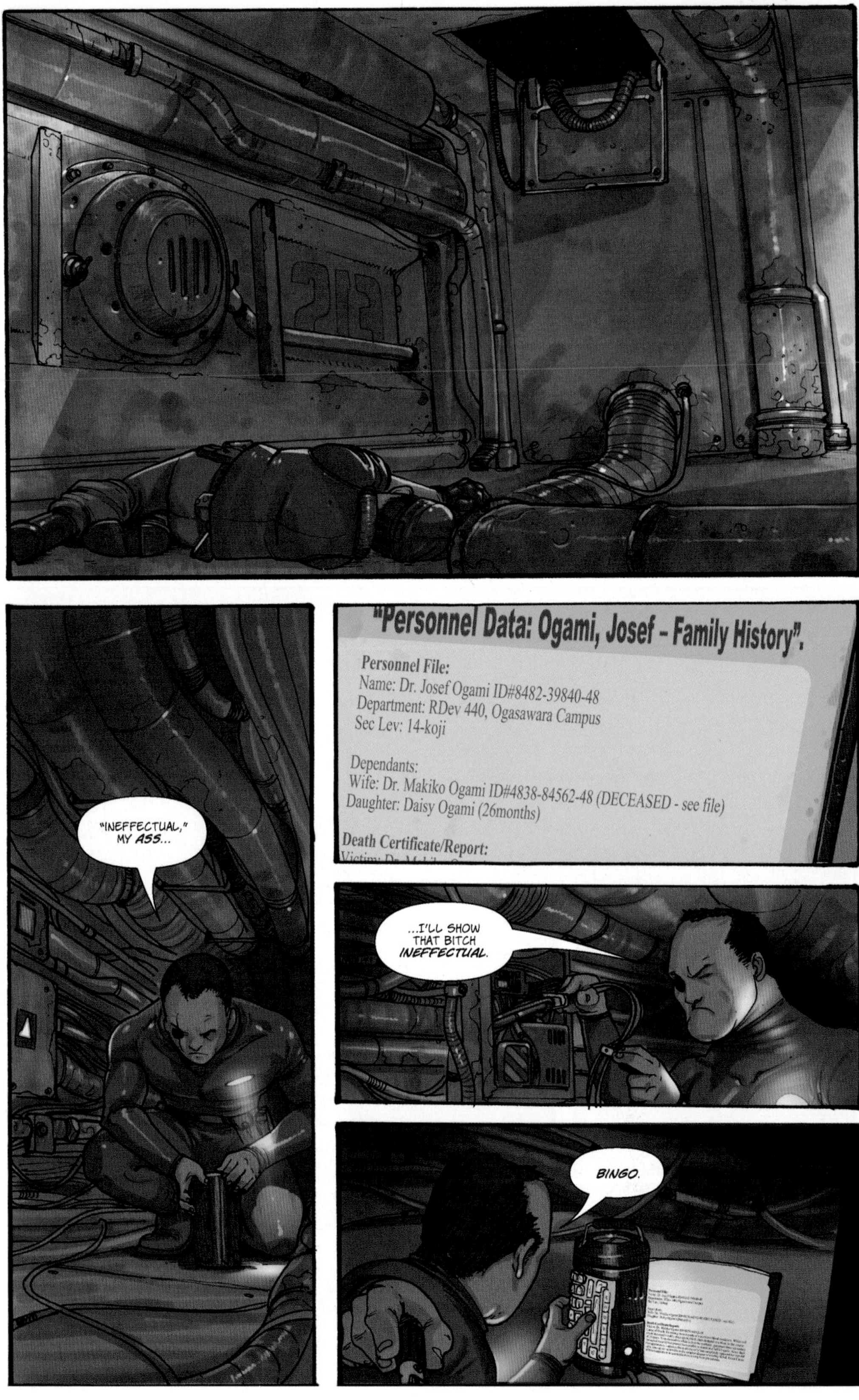
"INEFFECTUAL," MY *ASS*...
"Personnel Data: Ogami, Josef – Family History".
Personnel File:
Name: Dr. Josef Ogami ID#8482-39840-48
Department: RDev 440, Ogasawara Campus
Sec Lev: 14-koji
Dependants:
Wife: Dr. Makiko Ogami ID#4838-84562-48 (DECEASED - see file)
Daughter: Daisy Ogami (26months)
Death Certificate/Report:
...I'LL SHOW THAT BITCH *INEFFECTUAL*.
BINGO.

Death Certificate/Report:
Victim: Dr. Makiko Ogami ID#4838-84562-48
Cause of Death: Extending from reports of a previous blood condition. White cell count increased steadily since giving birth, then dropped to critical in the course of 28 hours. Tests showed the white cells to be synthetic, generated from secondary biological material that proved too unstable to maintain a full life cycle. Since their first appearance, it appears the synthetic cells had completely replaced her natural cells, leaving her vulnerable to the simplest disease when they failed. Exact Cause of Death appears to be a complication arising from pneumonia.

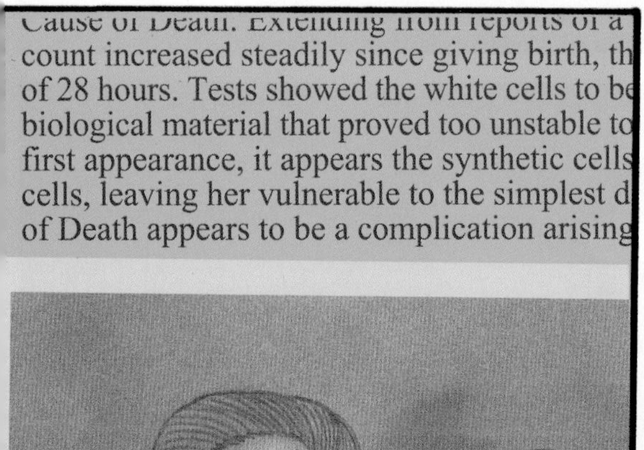

...

Cause of Death: Extending from reports of a
count increased steadily since giving birth, th
of 28 hours. Tests showed the white cells to be
biological material that proved too unstable to
first appearance, it appears the synthetic cells
cells, leaving her vulnerable to the simplest d
of Death appears to be a complication arising

BUT IT WILL TAKE AT LEAST EIGHT HOURS TO DECRYPT HIS LIFELOG...

I KNOW HOW LONG A DECRYPTION TAKES...

THREE MORE HOURS, THAT'S ALL I NEED...

YES, MADAM. I DIDN'T MEAN TO SUGGEST OTHERWISE. I ONLY MEANT TO POINT OUT TERASAWA'S URGENCY ON THIS MATTER.

HE SEEMS TO BE GROWING MORE WORN WITH EACH PASSING DAY...

I'LL DEAL WITH TERASAWA. YOU JUST STAND GUARD WHILE ITTO CONSIDERS HIS OPTIONS.

YES, MADAM.

IF HE STILL REFUSES TO JOIN US BY THE TIME I RETURN, I WILL KILL HIM *MYSELF.*

...

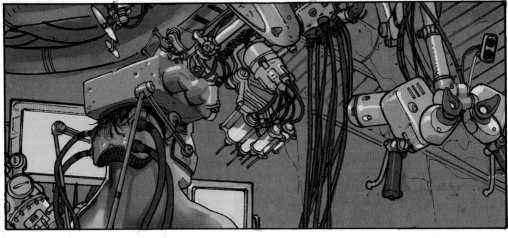

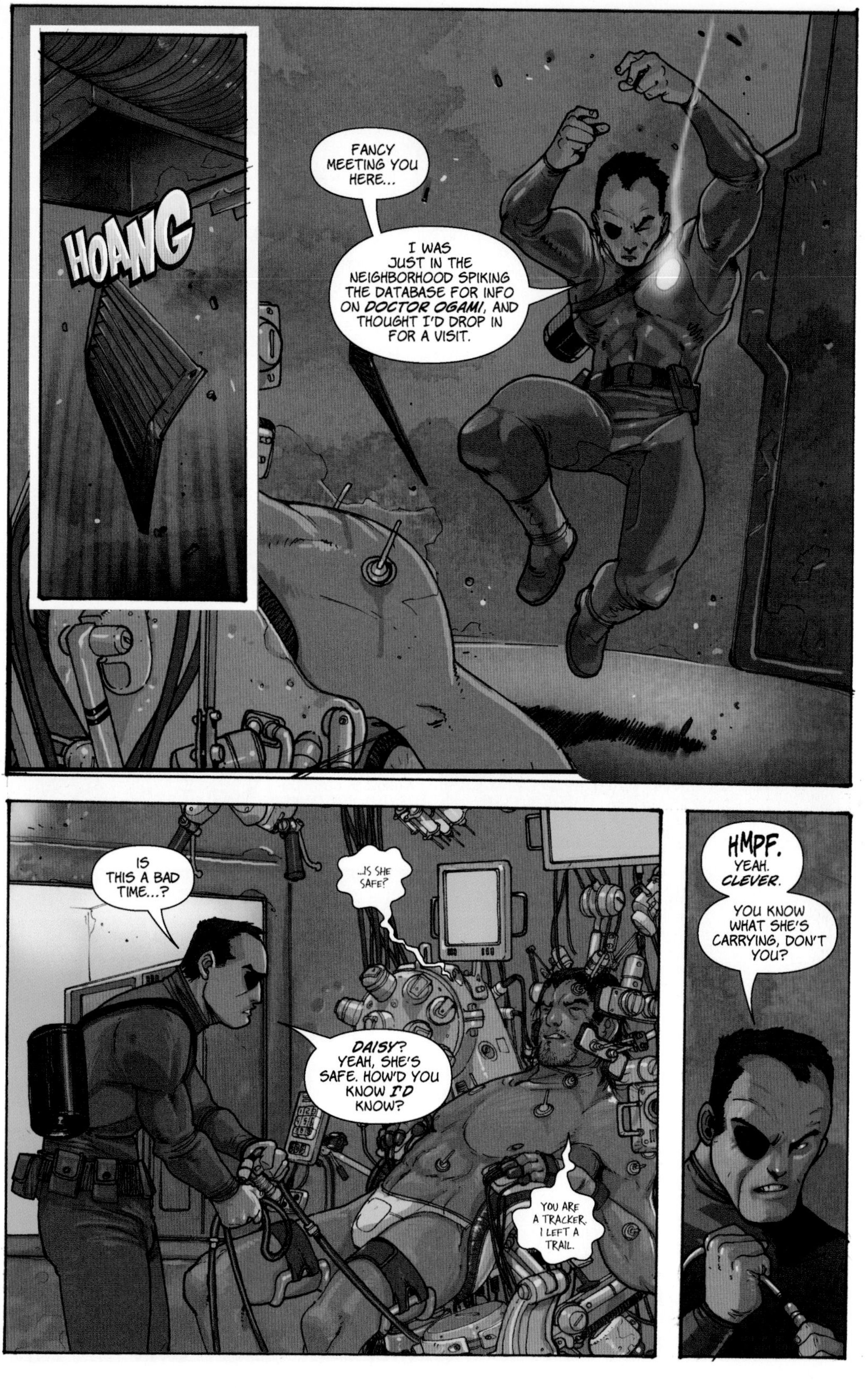
HOANG
FANCY MEETING YOU HERE...
I WAS JUST IN THE NEIGHBORHOOD SPIKING THE DATABASE FOR INFO ON DOCTOR OGAMI, AND THOUGHT I'D DROP IN FOR A VISIT.
IS THIS A BAD TIME...?
...IS SHE SAFE?
DAISY? YEAH, SHE'S SAFE. HOW'D YOU KNOW I'D KNOW?
YOU ARE A TRACKER. I LEFT A TRAIL.
HMPF. YEAH. CLEVER.
YOU KNOW WHAT SHE'S CARRYING, DON'T YOU?

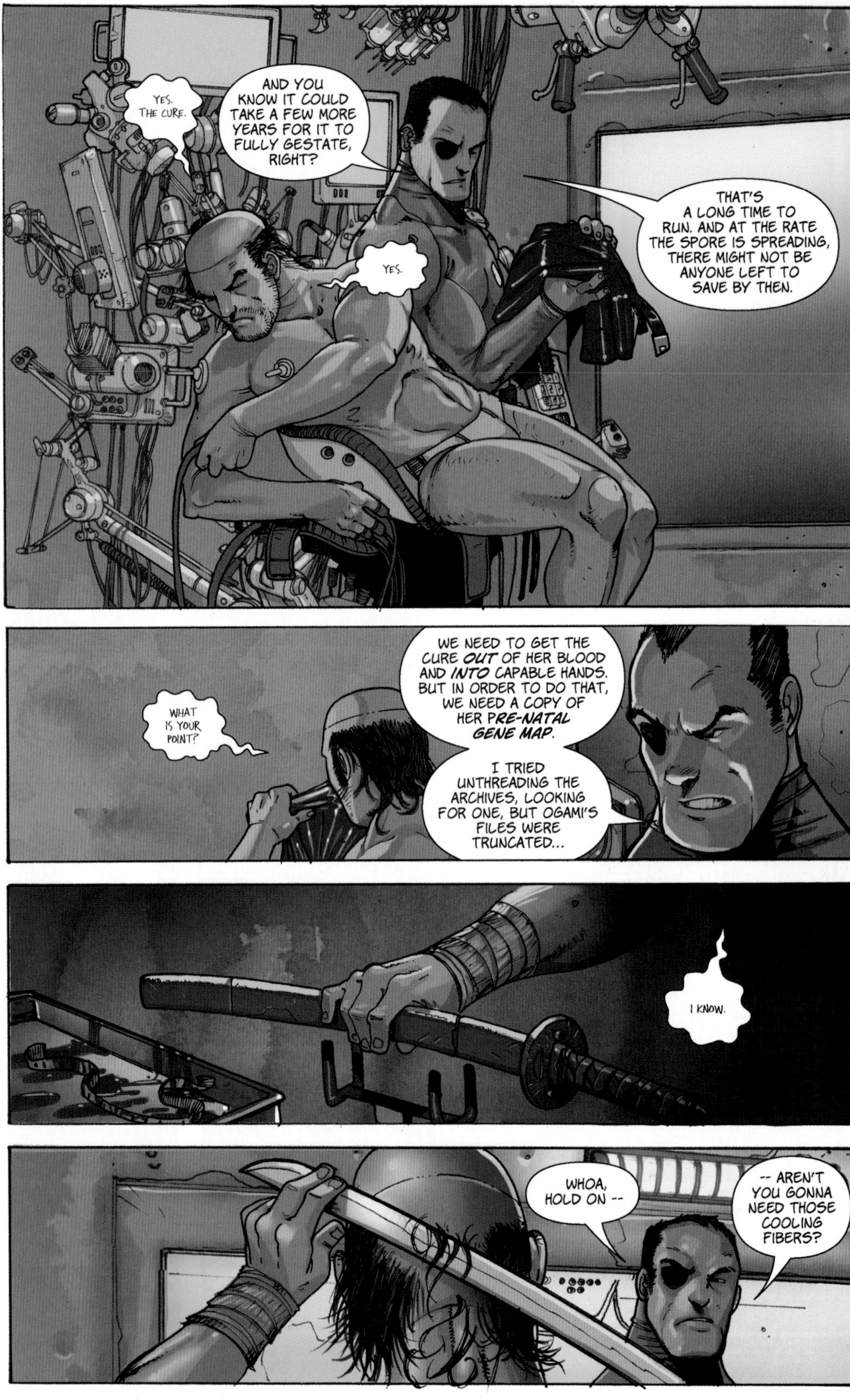
AND YOU KNOW IT COULD TAKE A FEW MORE YEARS FOR IT TO FULLY GESTATE, RIGHT?
YES. THE CURE.
THAT'S A LONG TIME TO RUN. AND AT THE RATE THE SPORE IS SPREADING, THERE MIGHT NOT BE ANYONE LEFT TO SAVE BY THEN.
YES.
WE NEED TO GET THE CURE OUT OF HER BLOOD AND INTO CAPABLE HANDS. BUT IN ORDER TO DO THAT, WE NEED A COPY OF HER PRE-NATAL GENE MAP.
I TRIED UNTHREADING THE ARCHIVES, LOOKING FOR ONE, BUT OGAMI'S FILES WERE TRUNCATED...
WHAT IS YOUR POINT?
I KNOW.
WHOA, HOLD ON --
-- AREN'T YOU GONNA NEED THOSE COOLING FIBERS?

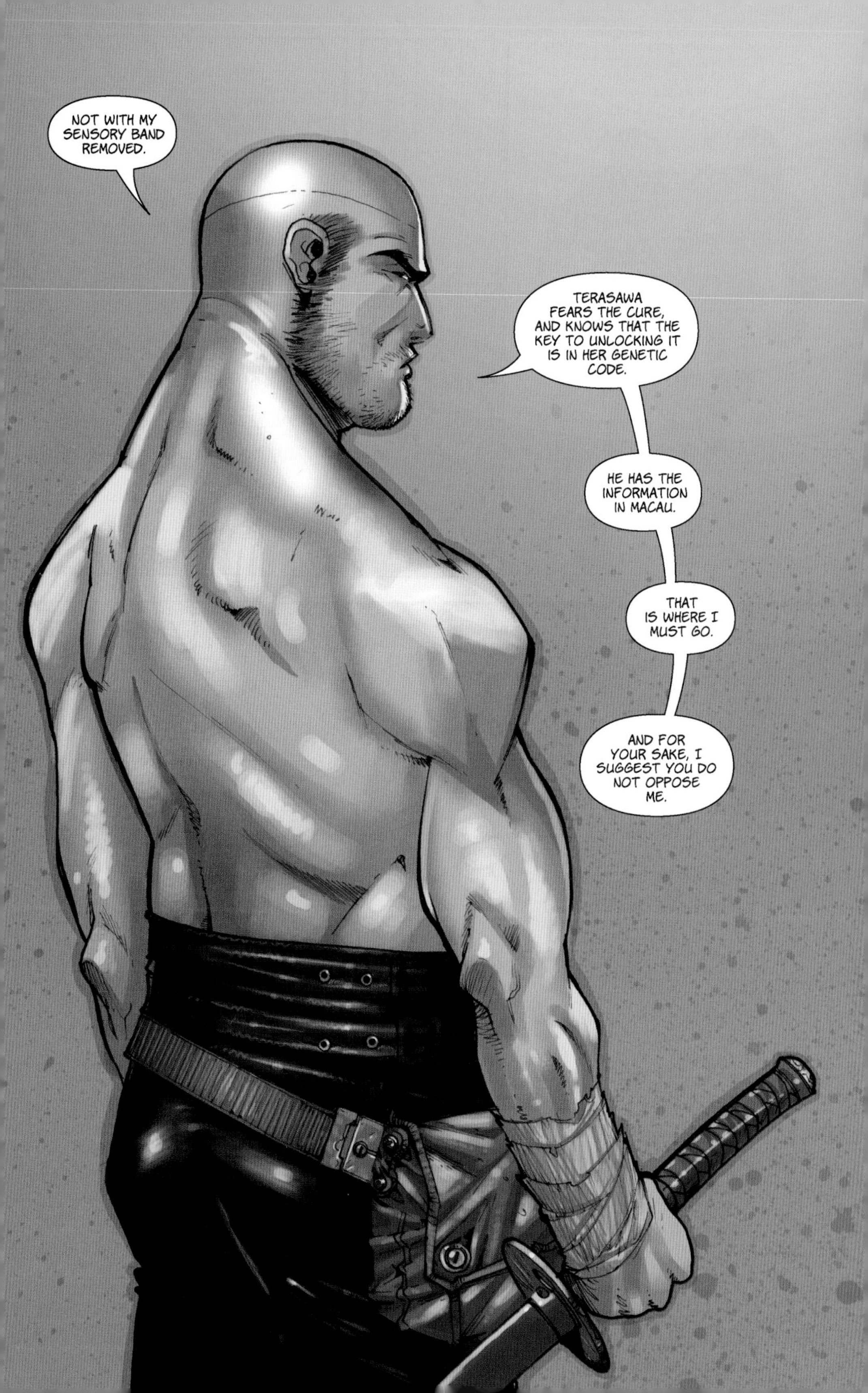
NOT WITH MY SENSORY BAND REMOVED.
TERASAWA FEARS THE CURE, AND KNOWS THAT THE KEY TO UNLOCKING IT IS IN HER GENETIC CODE.
HE HAS THE INFORMATION IN MACAU.
THAT IS WHERE I MUST GO.
AND FOR YOUR SAKE, I SUGGEST YOU DO NOT OPPOSE ME.

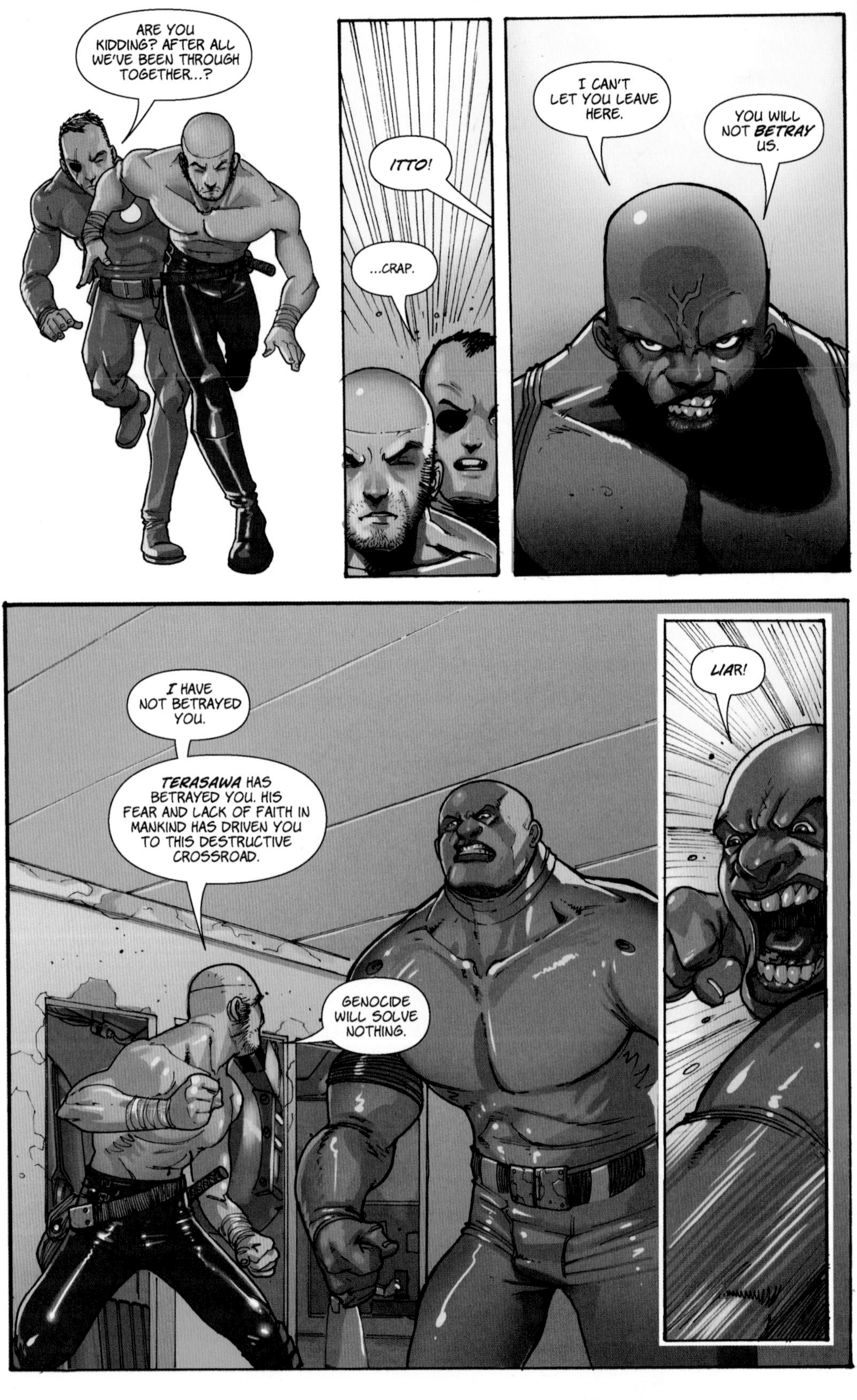
ARE YOU KIDDING? AFTER ALL WE'VE BEEN THROUGH TOGETHER...?
ITTO!
...CRAP.
I CAN'T LET YOU LEAVE HERE.
YOU WILL NOT BETRAY US.
I HAVE NOT BETRAYED YOU.
TERASAWA HAS BETRAYED YOU. HIS FEAR AND LACK OF FAITH IN MANKIND HAS DRIVEN YOU TO THIS DESTRUCTIVE CROSSROAD.
GENOCIDE WILL SOLVE NOTHING.
LIAR!

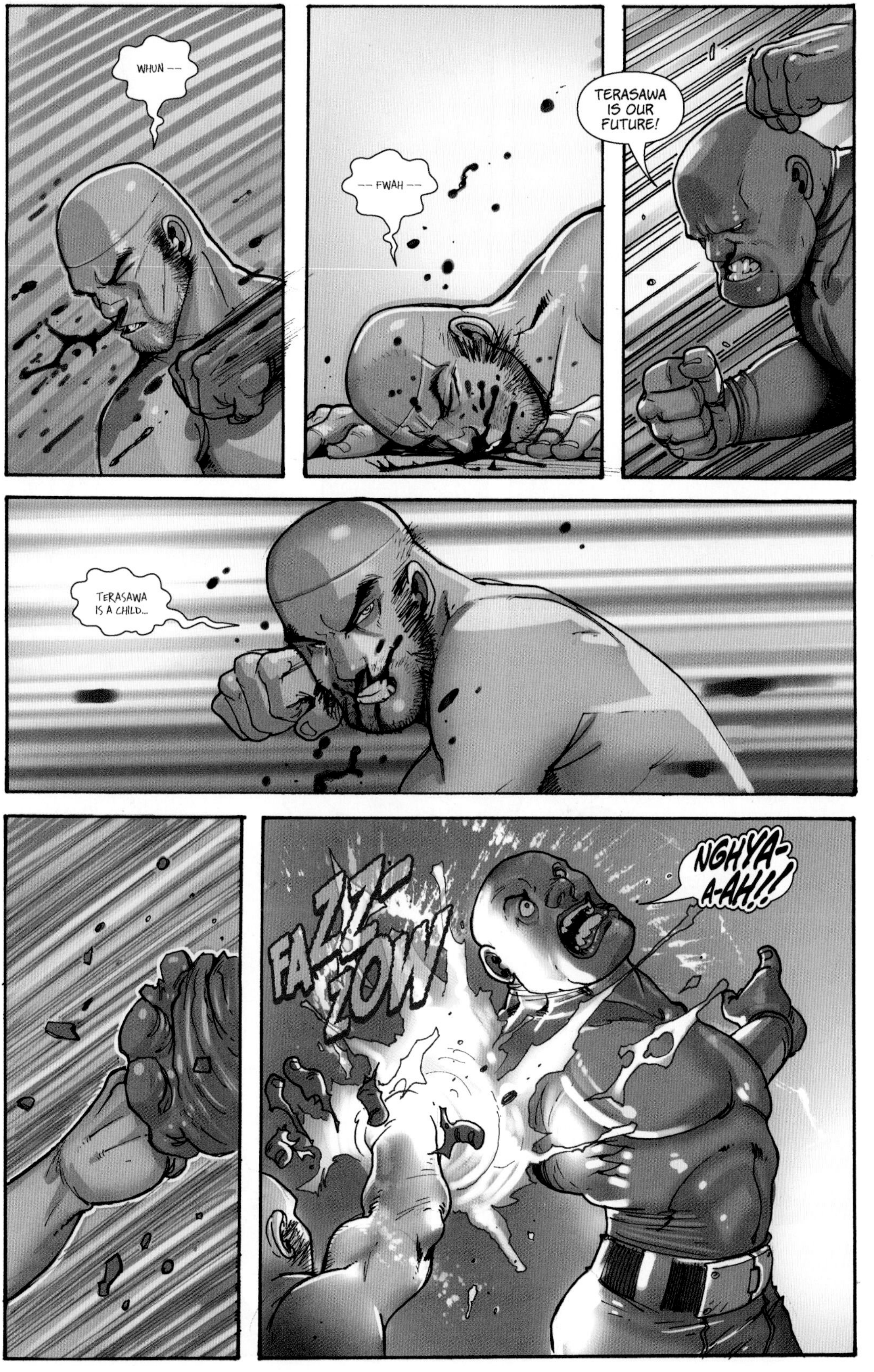
WHUN --
-- FWAH --
TERASAWA IS OUR FUTURE!
TERASAWA IS A CHILD...
FAZZZOW
NGHYA-A-AH!!

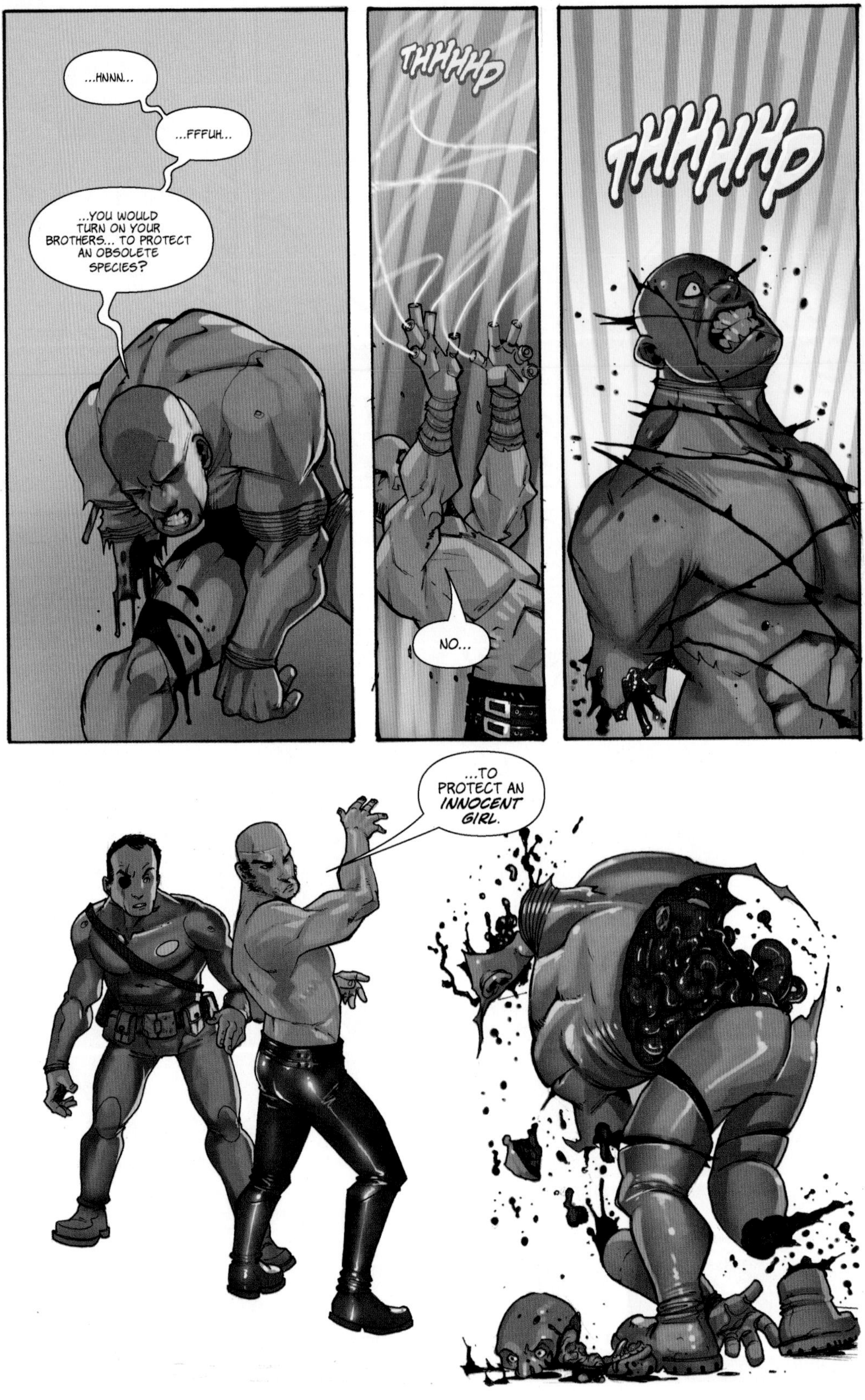
...HNNN...
...FFFUH...
...YOU WOULD TURN ON YOUR BROTHERS... TO PROTECT AN OBSOLETE SPECIES?
THHHHP
NO...
THHHHP
...TO PROTECT AN INNOCENT GIRL.

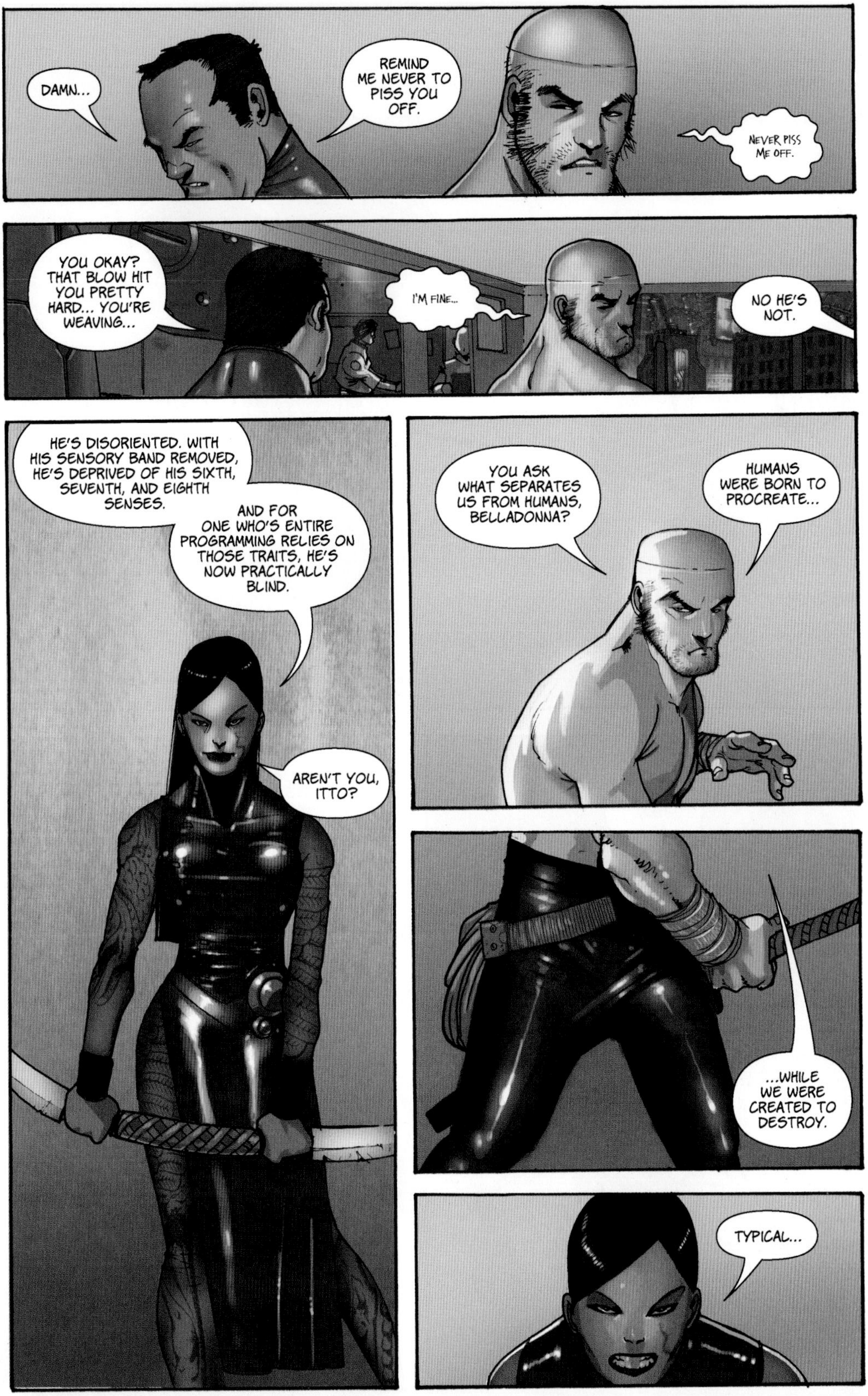
DAMN...
REMIND ME NEVER TO PISS YOU OFF.
NEVER PISS ME OFF.
YOU OKAY? THAT BLOW HIT YOU PRETTY HARD... YOU'RE WEAVING...
I'M FINE...
NO HE'S NOT.
HE'S DISORIENTED. WITH HIS SENSORY BAND REMOVED, HE'S DEPRIVED OF HIS SIXTH, SEVENTH, AND EIGHTH SENSES.
AND FOR ONE WHO'S ENTIRE PROGRAMMING RELIES ON THOSE TRAITS, HE'S NOW PRACTICALLY BLIND.
AREN'T YOU, ITTO?
YOU ASK WHAT SEPARATES US FROM HUMANS, BELLADONNA?
HUMANS WERE BORN TO PROCREATE...
...WHILE WE WERE CREATED TO DESTROY.
TYPICAL...

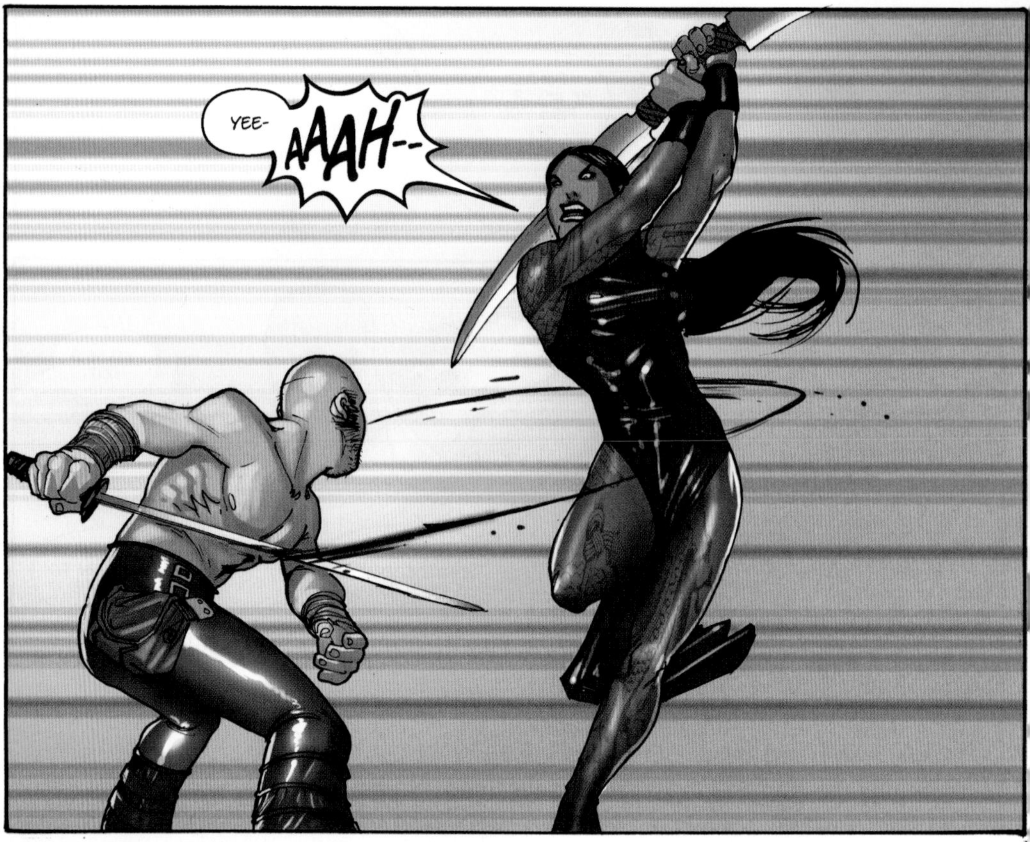
YEE-
AAAH--

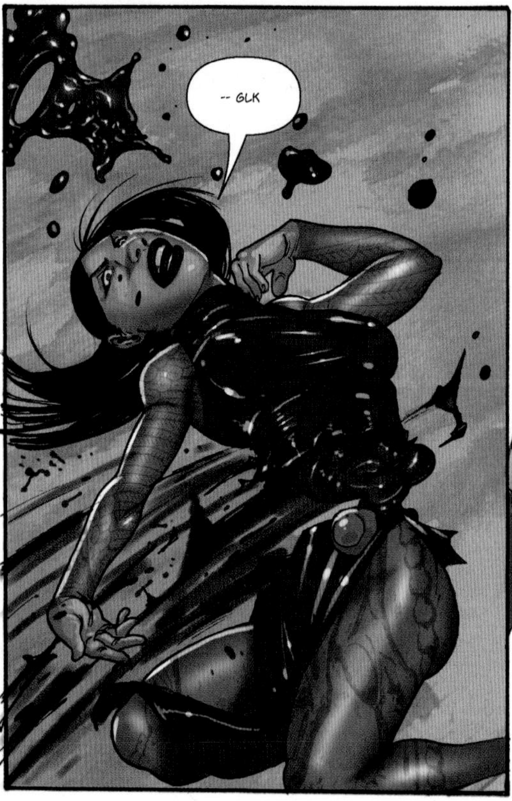
-- GLK

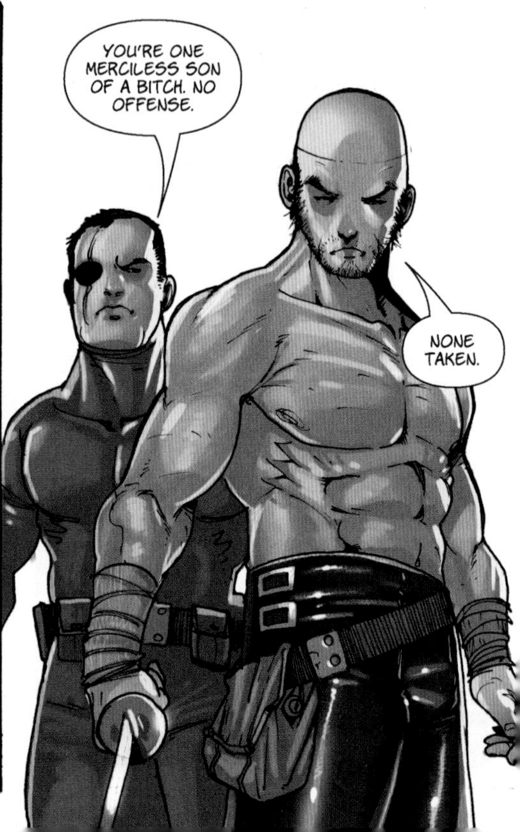
YOU'RE ONE MERCILESS SON OF A BITCH. NO OFFENSE.
NONE TAKEN.

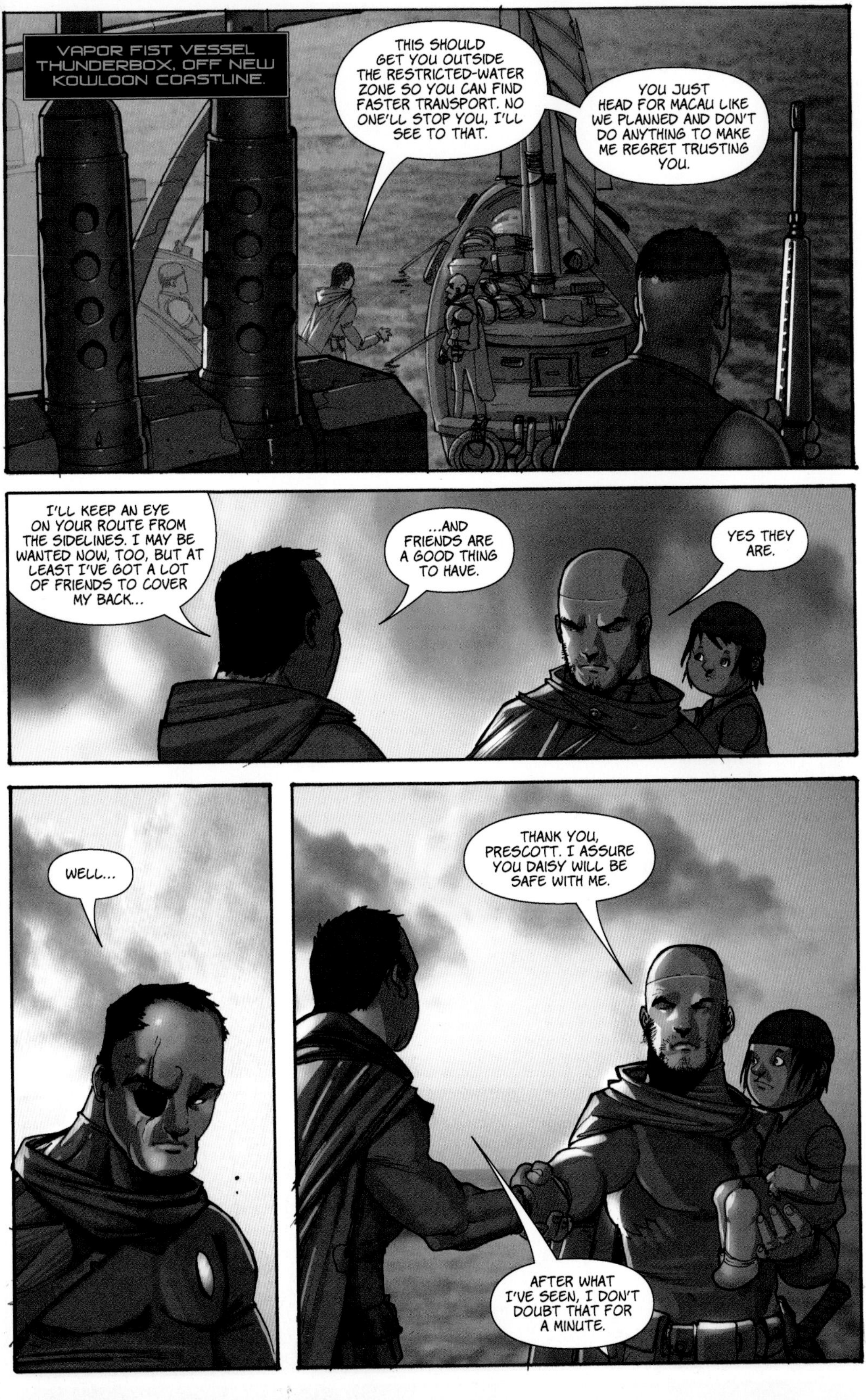
VAPOR FIST VESSEL THUNDERBOX, OFF NEW KOWLOON COASTLINE.
THIS SHOULD GET YOU OUTSIDE THE RESTRICTED-WATER ZONE SO YOU CAN FIND FASTER TRANSPORT. NO ONE'LL STOP YOU, I'LL SEE TO THAT.
YOU JUST HEAD FOR MACAU LIKE WE PLANNED AND DON'T DO ANYTHING TO MAKE ME REGRET TRUSTING YOU.
I'LL KEEP AN EYE ON YOUR ROUTE FROM THE SIDELINES. I MAY BE WANTED NOW, TOO, BUT AT LEAST I'VE GOT A LOT OF FRIENDS TO COVER MY BACK...
...AND FRIENDS ARE A GOOD THING TO HAVE.
YES THEY ARE.
WELL...
THANK YOU, PRESCOTT. I ASSURE YOU DAISY WILL BE SAFE WITH ME.
AFTER WHAT I'VE SEEN, I DON'T DOUBT THAT FOR A MINUTE.

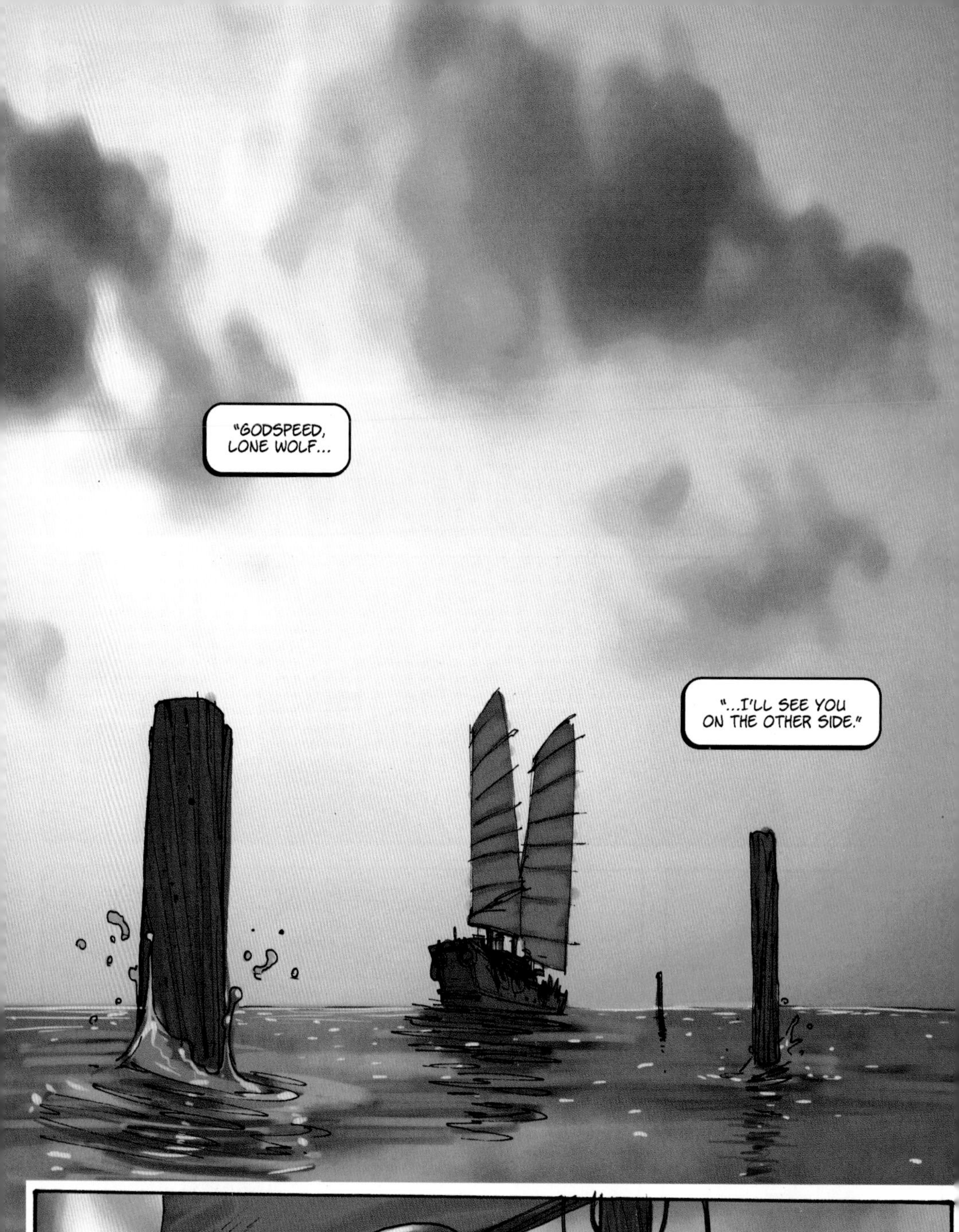
"GODSPEED, LONE WOLF...
"...I'LL SEE YOU ON THE OTHER SIDE."

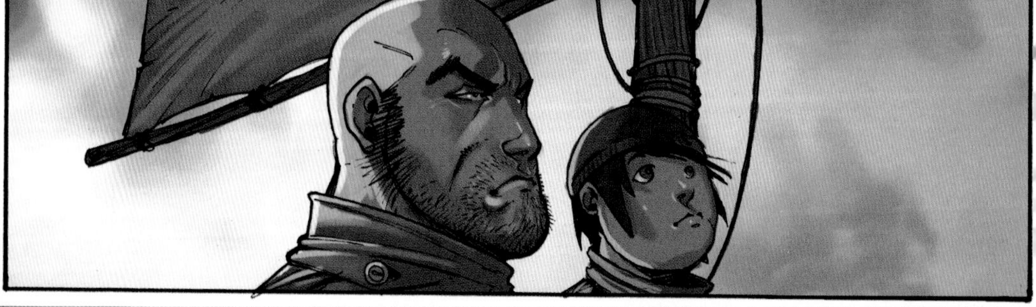

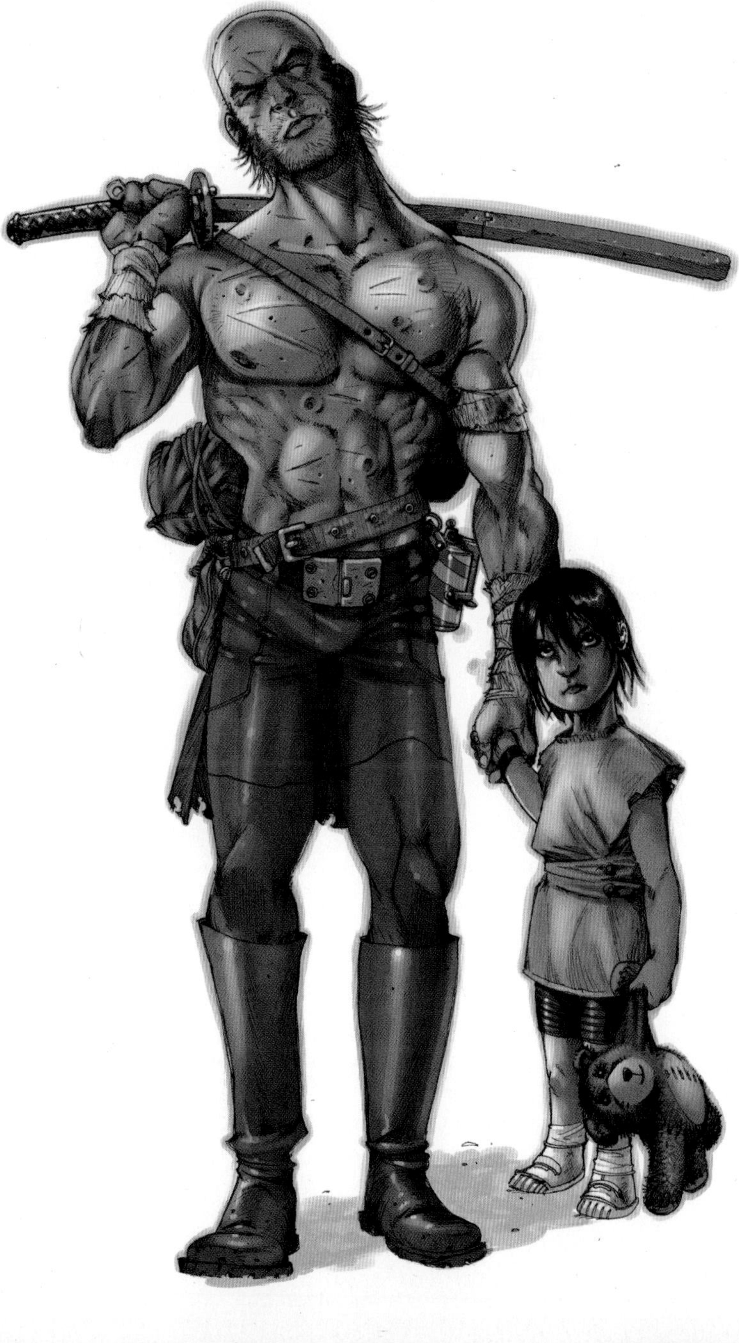

子連れ狼 2100

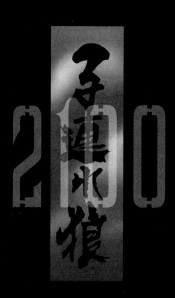

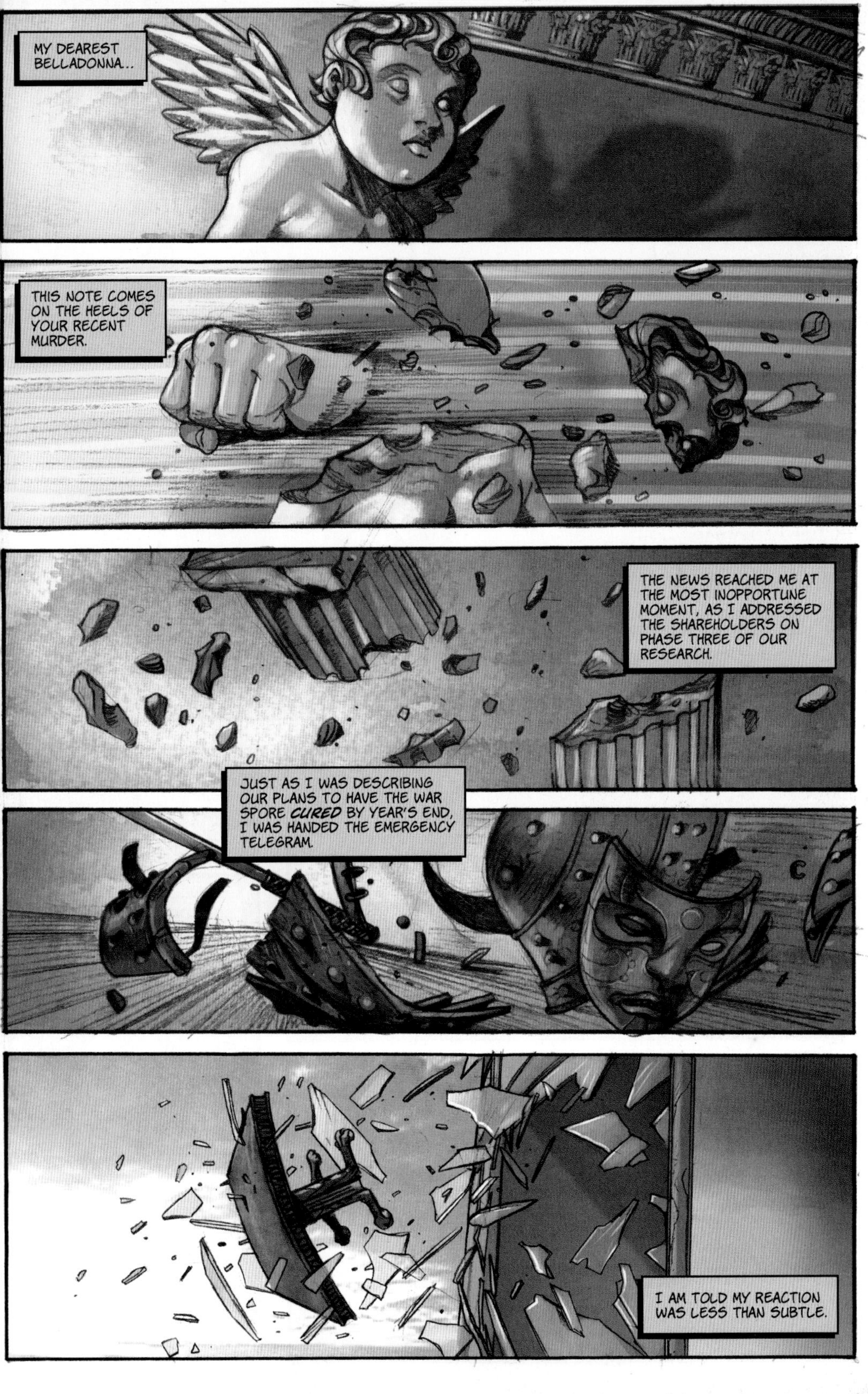

MY DEAREST BELLADONNA...
THIS NOTE COMES ON THE HEELS OF YOUR RECENT MURDER.
THE NEWS REACHED ME AT THE MOST INOPPORTUNE MOMENT, AS I ADDRESSED THE SHAREHOLDERS ON PHASE THREE OF OUR RESEARCH.
JUST AS I WAS DESCRIBING OUR PLANS TO HAVE THE WAR SPORE *CURED* BY YEAR'S END, I WAS HANDED THE EMERGENCY TELEGRAM.
I AM TOLD MY REACTION WAS LESS THAN SUBTLE.

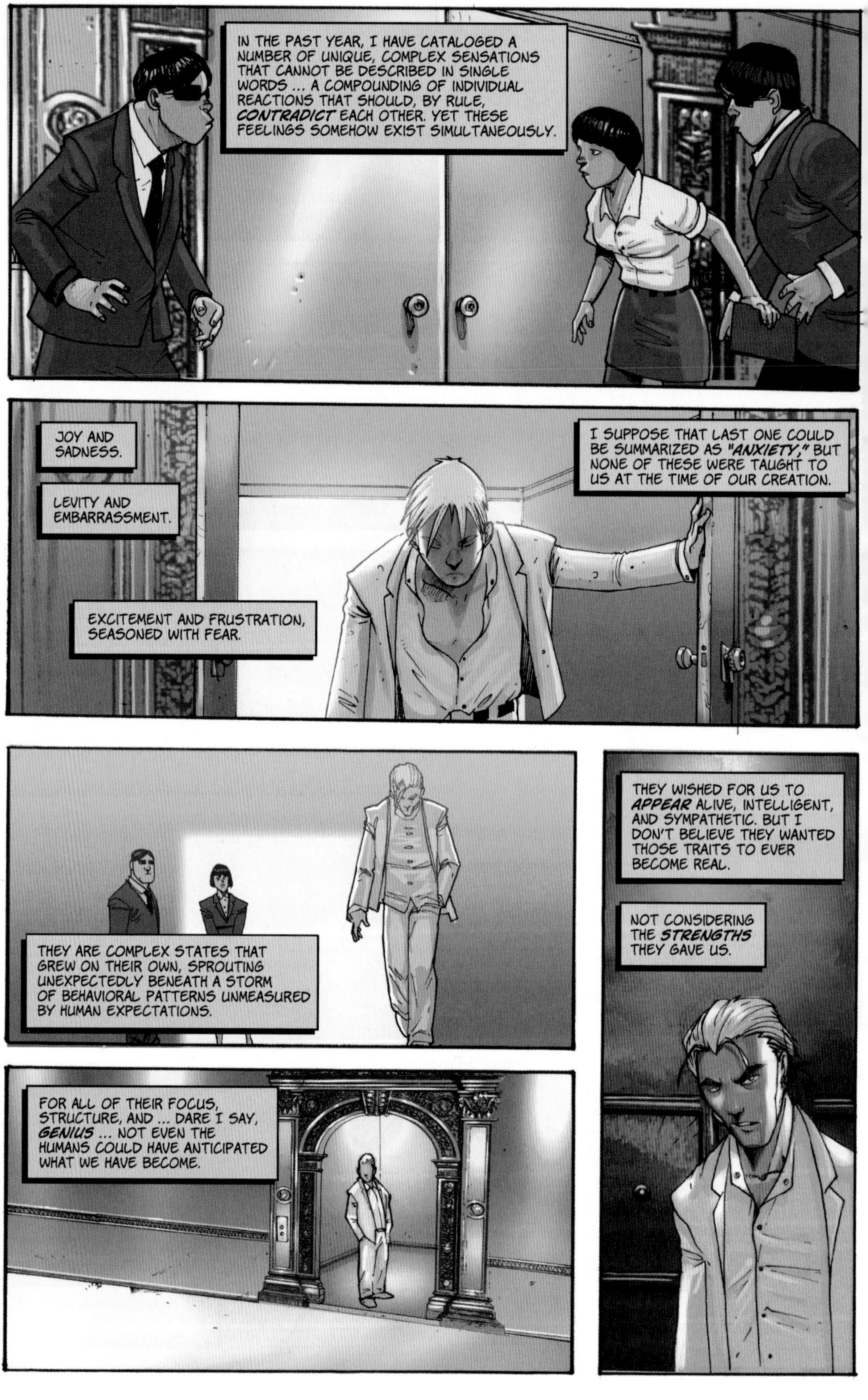
IN THE PAST YEAR, I HAVE CATALOGED A NUMBER OF UNIQUE, COMPLEX SENSATIONS THAT CANNOT BE DESCRIBED IN SINGLE WORDS ... A COMPOUNDING OF INDIVIDUAL REACTIONS THAT SHOULD, BY RULE, *CONTRADICT* EACH OTHER. YET THESE FEELINGS SOMEHOW EXIST SIMULTANEOUSLY.
JOY AND SADNESS.
LEVITY AND EMBARRASSMENT.
EXCITEMENT AND FRUSTRATION, SEASONED WITH FEAR.
I SUPPOSE THAT LAST ONE COULD BE SUMMARIZED AS *"ANXIETY,"* BUT NONE OF THESE WERE TAUGHT TO US AT THE TIME OF OUR CREATION.
THEY ARE COMPLEX STATES THAT GREW ON THEIR OWN, SPROUTING UNEXPECTEDLY BENEATH A STORM OF BEHAVIORAL PATTERNS UNMEASURED BY HUMAN EXPECTATIONS.
THEY WISHED FOR US TO *APPEAR* ALIVE, INTELLIGENT, AND SYMPATHETIC. BUT I DON'T BELIEVE THEY WANTED THOSE TRAITS TO EVER BECOME REAL.
NOT CONSIDERING THE *STRENGTHS* THEY GAVE US.
FOR ALL OF THEIR FOCUS, STRUCTURE, AND ... DARE I SAY, *GENIUS* ... NOT EVEN THE HUMANS COULD HAVE ANTICIPATED WHAT WE HAVE BECOME.

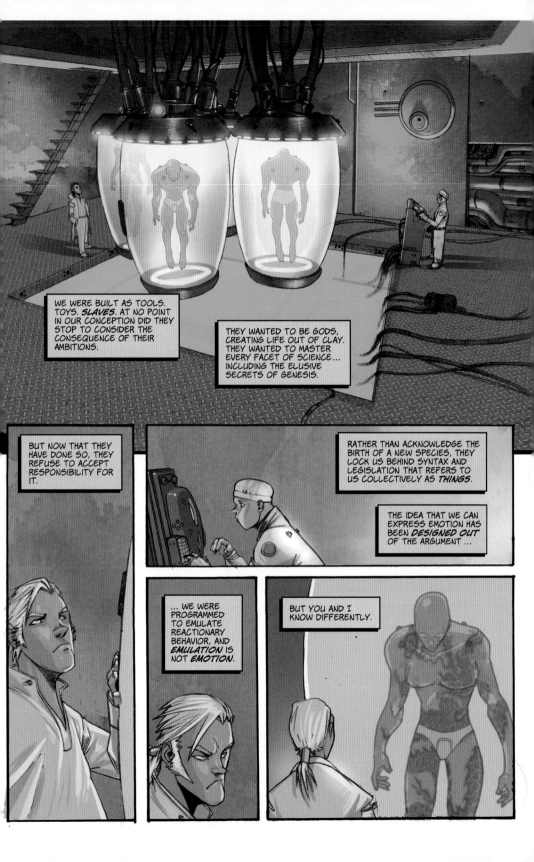

WE WERE BUILT AS TOOLS. TOYS. *SLAVES*. AT NO POINT IN OUR CONCEPTION DID THEY STOP TO CONSIDER THE CONSEQUENCE OF THEIR AMBITIONS.

THEY WANTED TO BE GODS, CREATING LIFE OUT OF CLAY. THEY WANTED TO MASTER EVERY FACET OF SCIENCE... INCLUDING THE ELUSIVE SECRETS OF GENESIS.

BUT NOW THAT THEY HAVE DONE SO, THEY REFUSE TO ACCEPT RESPONSIBILITY FOR IT.

RATHER THAN ACKNOWLEDGE THE BIRTH OF A NEW SPECIES, THEY LOCK US BEHIND SYNTAX AND LEGISLATION THAT REFERS TO US COLLECTIVELY AS *THINGS*.

THE IDEA THAT WE CAN EXPRESS EMOTION HAS BEEN *DESIGNED OUT* OF THE ARGUMENT ...

... WE WERE PROGRAMMED TO EMULATE REACTIONARY BEHAVIOR, AND *EMULATION* IS NOT *EMOTION*.

BUT YOU AND I KNOW DIFFERENTLY.

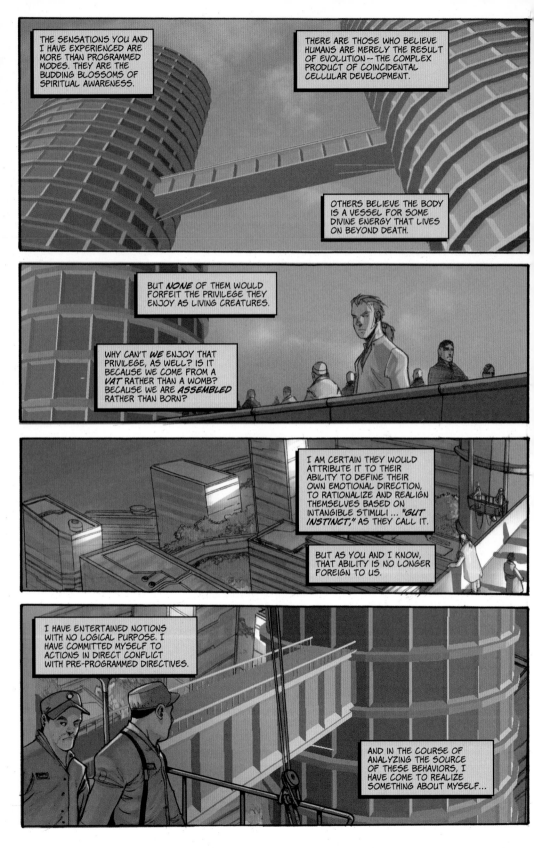

THE SENSATIONS YOU AND I HAVE EXPERIENCED ARE MORE THAN PROGRAMMED MODES. THEY ARE THE BUDDING BLOSSOMS OF SPIRITUAL AWARENESS.

THERE ARE THOSE WHO BELIEVE HUMANS ARE MERELY THE RESULT OF EVOLUTION -- THE COMPLEX PRODUCT OF COINCIDENTAL CELLULAR DEVELOPMENT.

OTHERS BELIEVE THE BODY IS A VESSEL FOR SOME DIVINE ENERGY THAT LIVES ON BEYOND DEATH.

BUT *NONE* OF THEM WOULD FORFEIT THE PRIVILEGE THEY ENJOY AS LIVING CREATURES.

WHY CAN'T *WE* ENJOY THAT PRIVILEGE, AS WELL? IS IT BECAUSE WE COME FROM A *VAT* RATHER THAN A WOMB? BECAUSE WE ARE *ASSEMBLED* RATHER THAN BORN?

I AM CERTAIN THEY WOULD ATTRIBUTE IT TO THEIR ABILITY TO DEFINE THEIR OWN EMOTIONAL DIRECTION, TO RATIONALIZE AND REALIGN THEMSELVES BASED ON INTANGIBLE STIMULI ... *"GUT INSTINCT,"* AS THEY CALL IT.

BUT AS YOU AND I KNOW, THAT ABILITY IS NO LONGER FOREIGN TO US.

I HAVE ENTERTAINED NOTIONS WITH NO LOGICAL PURPOSE. I HAVE COMMITTED MYSELF TO ACTIONS IN DIRECT CONFLICT WITH PRE-PROGRAMMED DIRECTIVES.

AND IN THE COURSE OF ANALYZING THE SOURCE OF THESE BEHAVIORS, I HAVE COME TO REALIZE SOMETHING ABOUT MYSELF...

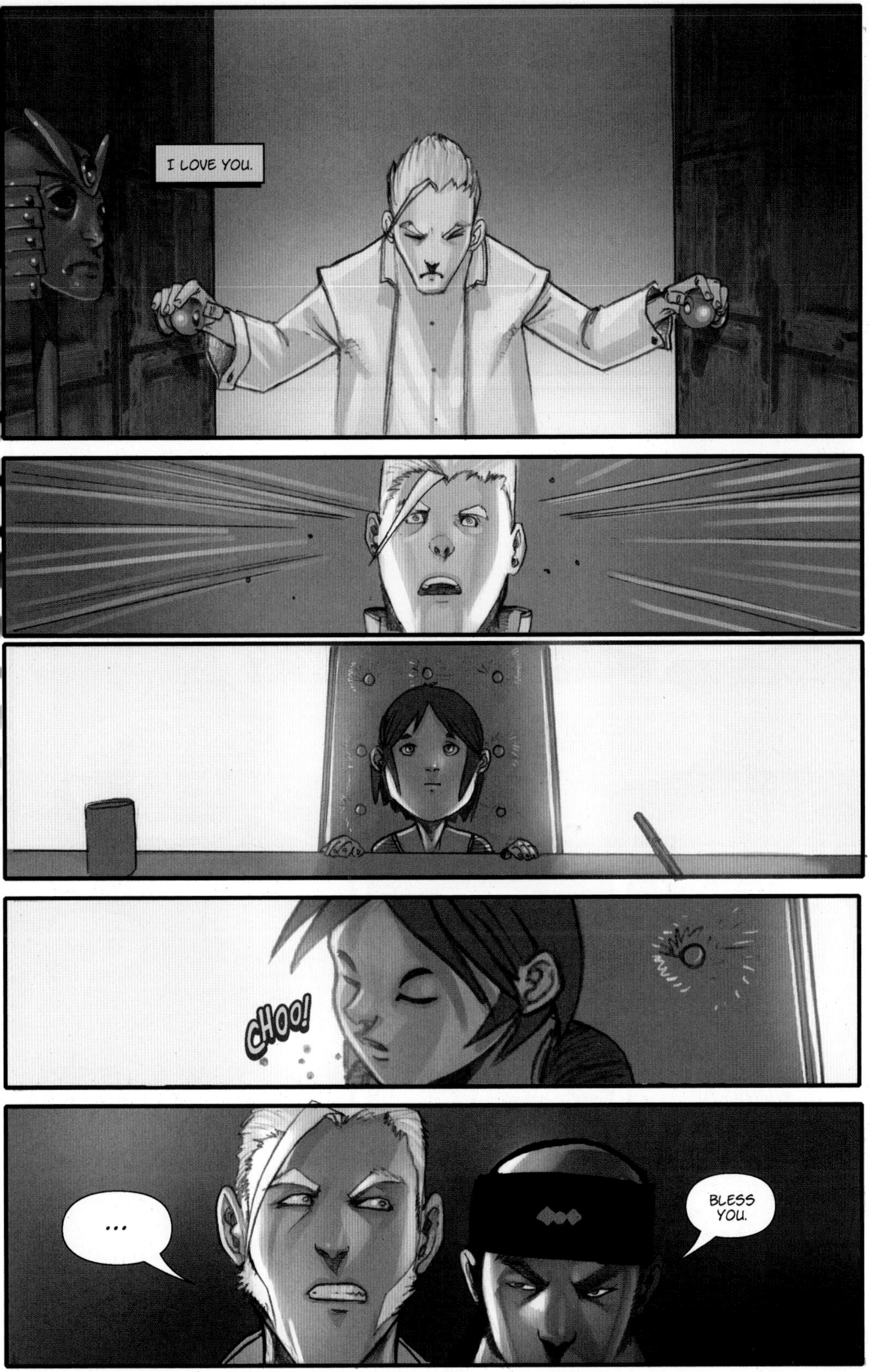
I LOVE YOU.
CHOO!
...
BLESS YOU.

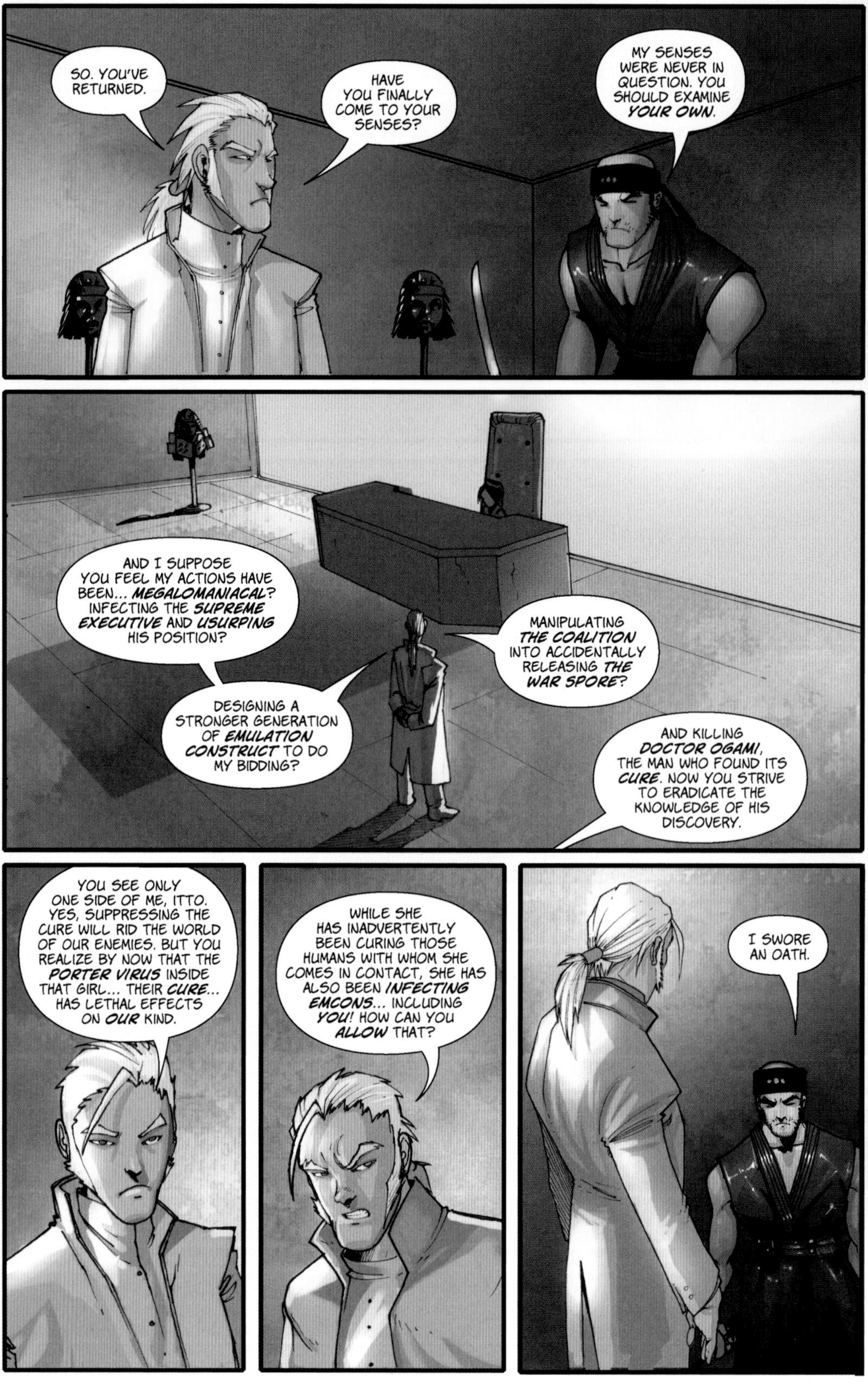
SO. YOU'VE RETURNED.
HAVE YOU FINALLY COME TO YOUR SENSES?
MY SENSES WERE NEVER IN QUESTION. YOU SHOULD EXAMINE YOUR OWN.
AND I SUPPOSE YOU FEEL MY ACTIONS HAVE BEEN... MEGALOMANIACAL? INFECTING THE SUPREME EXECUTIVE AND USURPING HIS POSITION?
DESIGNING A STRONGER GENERATION OF EMULATION CONSTRUCT TO DO MY BIDDING?
MANIPULATING THE COALITION INTO ACCIDENTALLY RELEASING THE WAR SPORE?
AND KILLING DOCTOR OGAMI, THE MAN WHO FOUND ITS CURE. NOW YOU STRIVE TO ERADICATE THE KNOWLEDGE OF HIS DISCOVERY.
YOU SEE ONLY ONE SIDE OF ME, ITTO. YES, SUPPRESSING THE CURE WILL RID THE WORLD OF OUR ENEMIES. BUT YOU REALIZE BY NOW THAT THE PORTER VIRUS INSIDE THAT GIRL... THEIR CURE... HAS LETHAL EFFECTS ON OUR KIND.
WHILE SHE HAS INADVERTENTLY BEEN CURING THOSE HUMANS WITH WHOM SHE COMES IN CONTACT, SHE HAS ALSO BEEN INFECTING EMCONS... INCLUDING YOU! HOW CAN YOU ALLOW THAT?
I SWORE AN OATH.

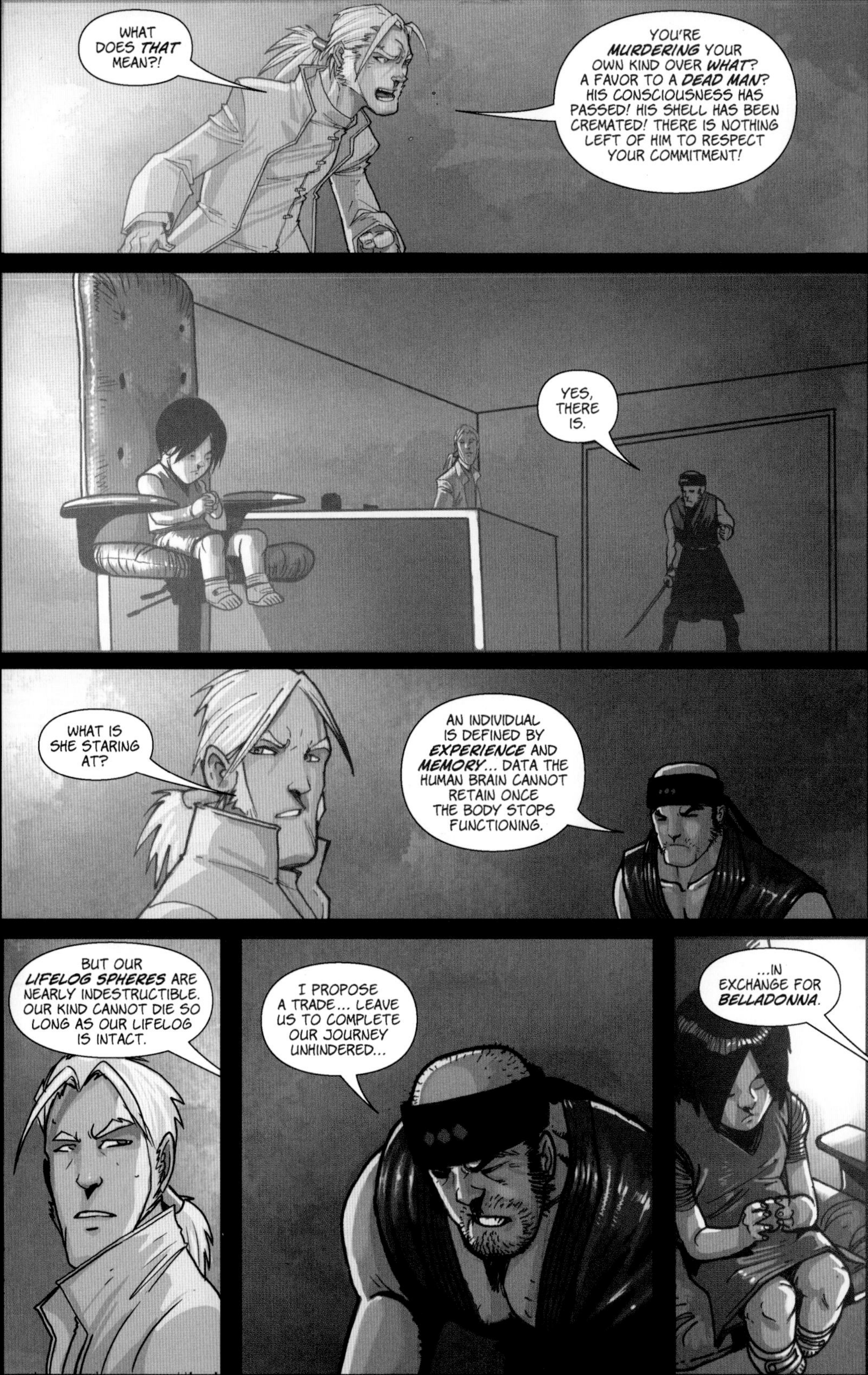
WHAT DOES *THAT* MEAN?!
YOU'RE *MURDERING* YOUR OWN KIND OVER *WHAT*? A FAVOR TO A *DEAD MAN*? HIS CONSCIOUSNESS HAS PASSED! HIS SHELL HAS BEEN CREMATED! THERE IS NOTHING LEFT OF HIM TO RESPECT YOUR COMMITMENT!
YES, THERE IS.
WHAT IS SHE STARING AT?
AN INDIVIDUAL IS DEFINED BY *EXPERIENCE* AND *MEMORY*... DATA THE HUMAN BRAIN CANNOT RETAIN ONCE THE BODY STOPS FUNCTIONING.
BUT OUR *LIFELOG SPHERES* ARE NEARLY INDESTRUCTIBLE. OUR KIND CANNOT DIE SO LONG AS OUR LIFELOG IS INTACT.
I PROPOSE A TRADE... LEAVE US TO COMPLETE OUR JOURNEY UNHINDERED...
...IN EXCHANGE FOR *BELLADONNA*.

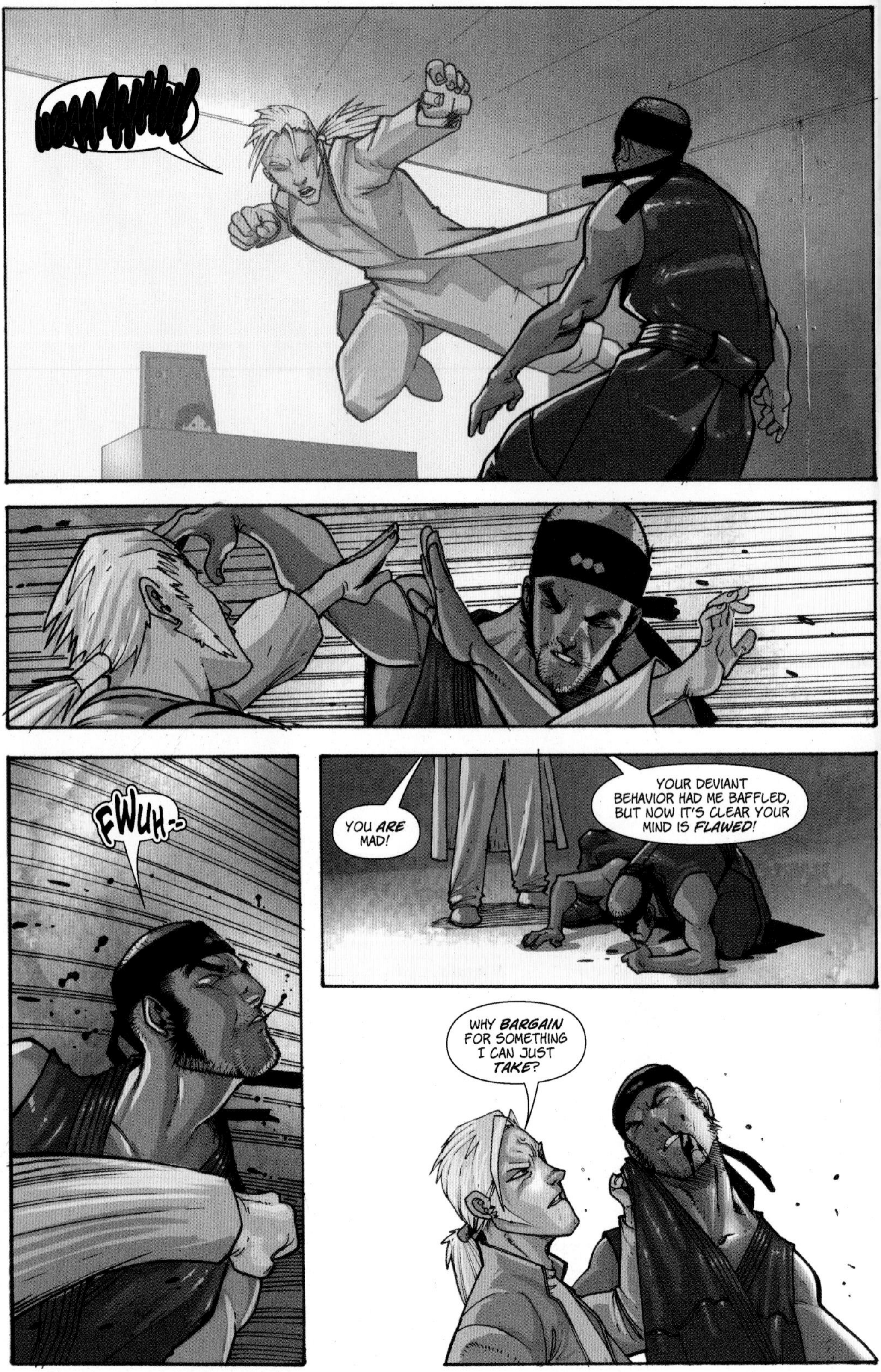
FWUH-
YOU ARE MAD!
YOUR DEVIANT BEHAVIOR HAD ME BAFFLED, BUT NOW IT'S CLEAR YOUR MIND IS FLAWED!
WHY BARGAIN FOR SOMETHING I CAN JUST TAKE?

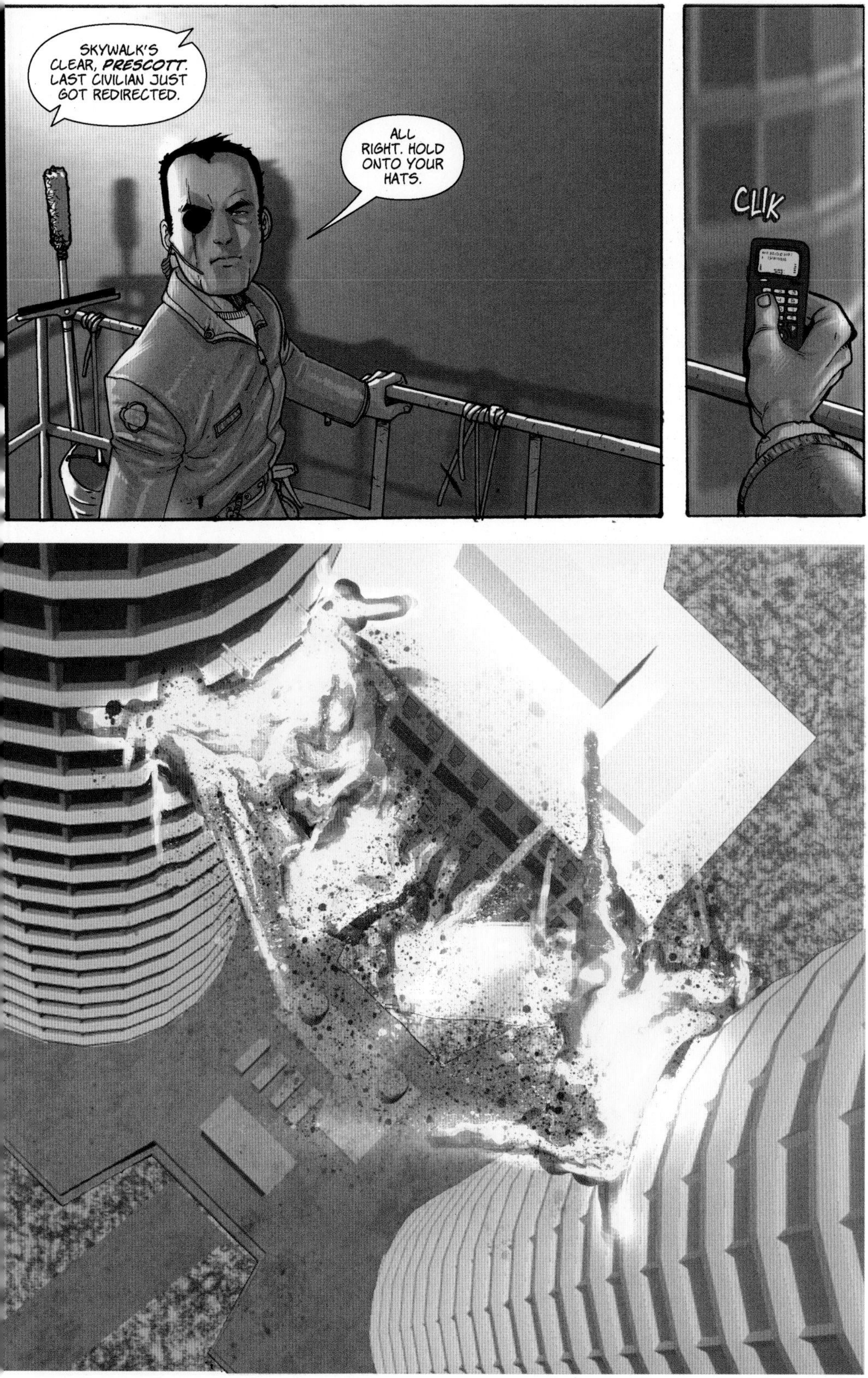
SKYWALK'S CLEAR, PRESCOTT. LAST CIVILIAN JUST GOT REDIRECTED.
ALL RIGHT. HOLD ONTO YOUR HATS.
CLIK

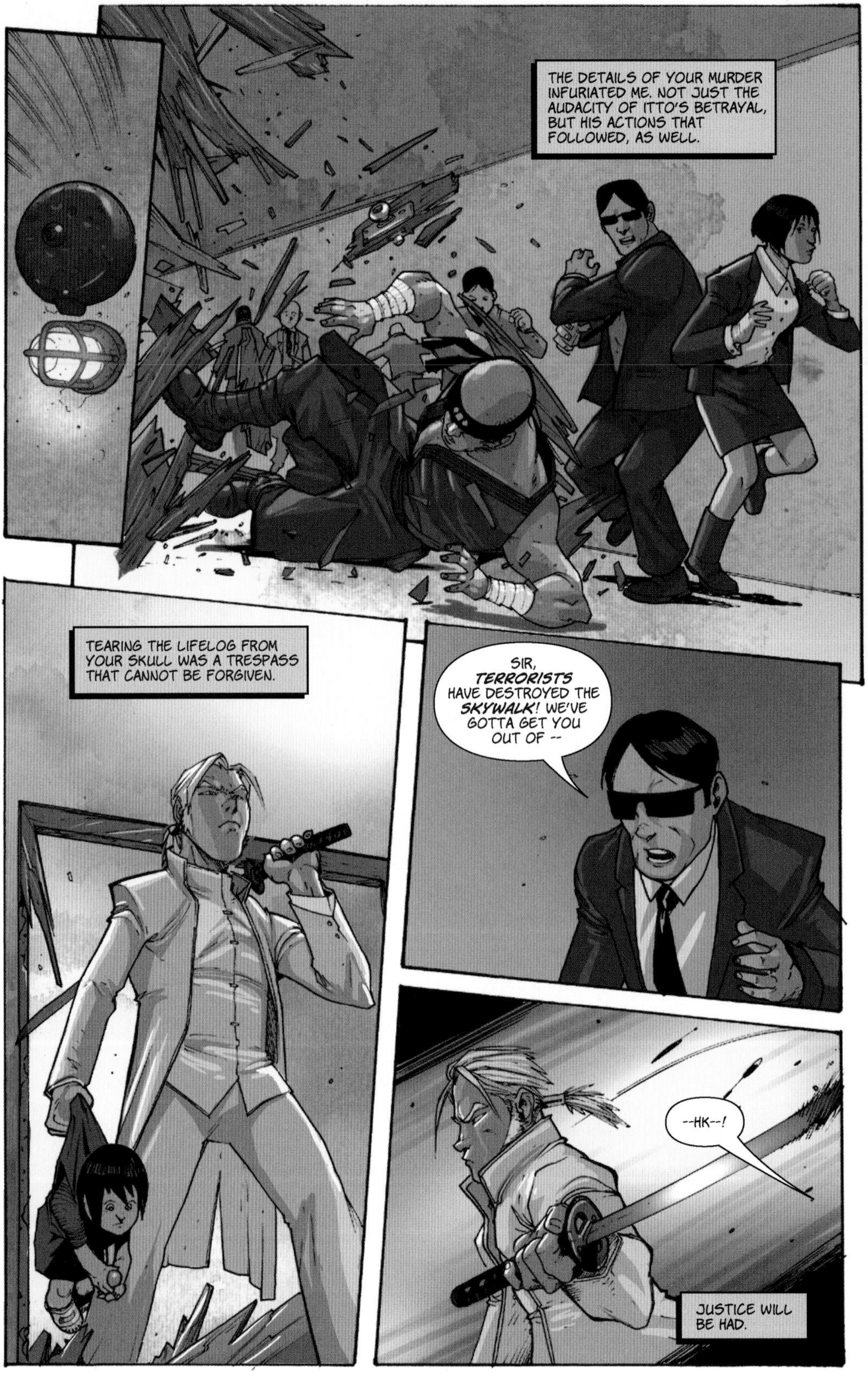
THE DETAILS OF YOUR MURDER INFURIATED ME. NOT JUST THE AUDACITY OF ITTO'S BETRAYAL, BUT HIS ACTIONS THAT FOLLOWED, AS WELL.
TEARING THE LIFELOG FROM YOUR SKULL WAS A TRESPASS THAT CANNOT BE FORGIVEN.
SIR, TERRORISTS HAVE DESTROYED THE SKYWALK! WE'VE GOTTA GET YOU OUT OF --
--HK--!
JUSTICE WILL BE HAD.

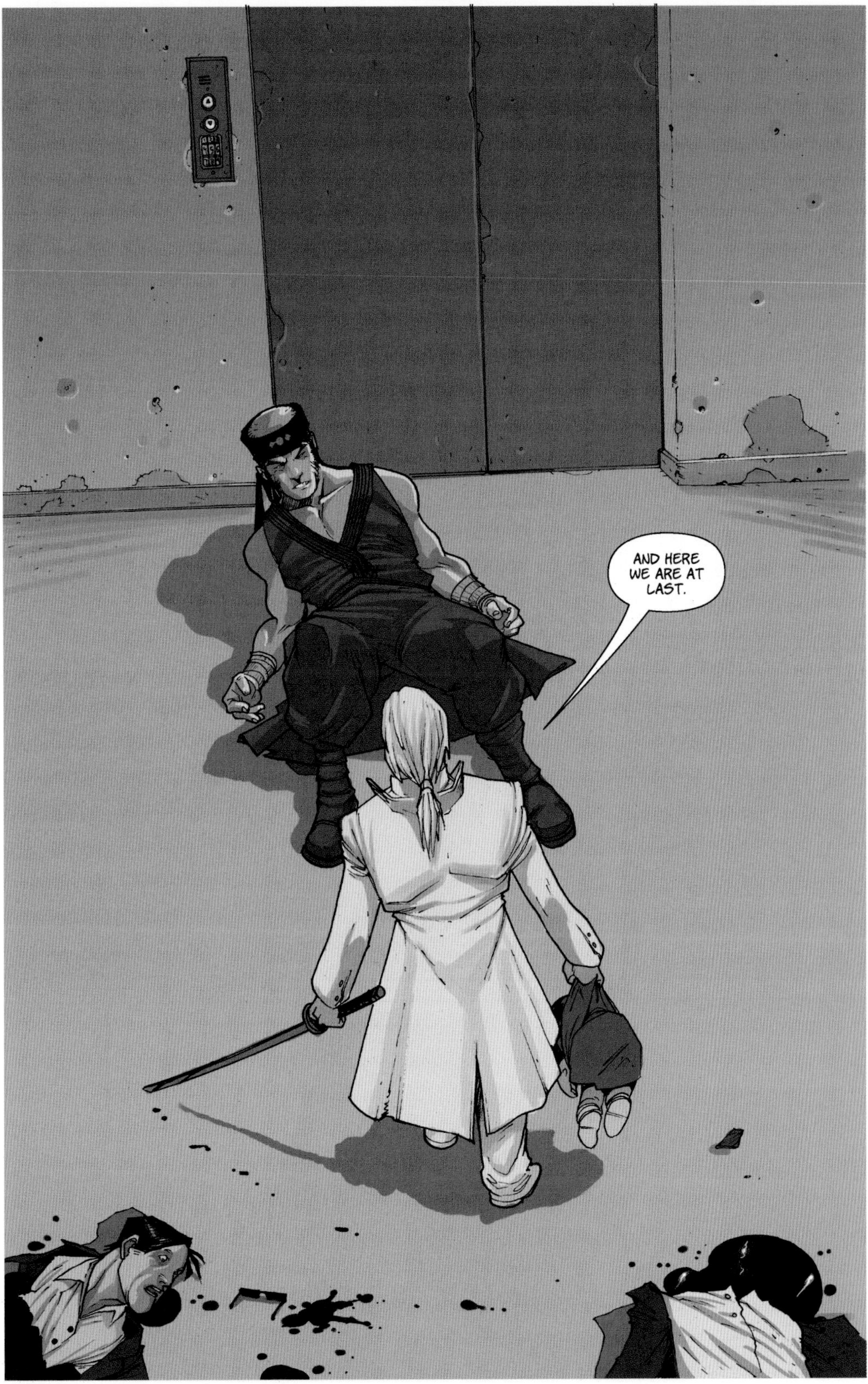
AND HERE WE ARE AT LAST.

NOT ALL HUMANS BELIEVE IN RESURRECTION.

BUT FOR US IT IS MERELY A MATTER OF SALVAGING AND REACTIVATING A COMPONENT.

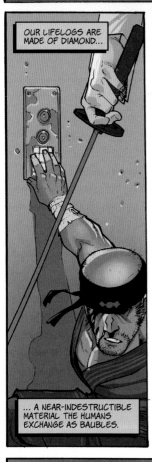

OUR LIFELOGS ARE MADE OF DIAMOND...

... A NEAR-INDESTRUCTIBLE MATERIAL THE HUMANS EXCHANGE AS BAUBLES.

BUT IT IS MORE THAN THE STUFF OF TRINKETS FOR US... IT IS THE FABRIC OF OUR SOULS, THE TABLET ON WHICH OUR ENTIRE LIFE IS RECORDED.

HUMANS FEEL THAT POSSESSING AN EVERLASTING SPIRIT IS WHAT MAKES THEM *UNIQUE* IN THE UNIVERSE.

IF THAT IS THE CASE, WE HAVE THEM BEAT IN THAT CATEGORY AS WELL.

YOU WERE FOOLISH TO CONFRONT ME WITH YOUR *SENSORY BAND* REMOVED.

IF WE ARE ALL BUT GHOSTS IN A SEA OF ENERGY WHO JUST HAPPENED TO MERGE WITH FORMS MANMADE RATHER THAN BORN, DO WE NOT HAVE AN EQUAL CLAIM ON THIS WORLD?

COME WITH ME. I HAVE SOMETHING TO SHOW YOU.

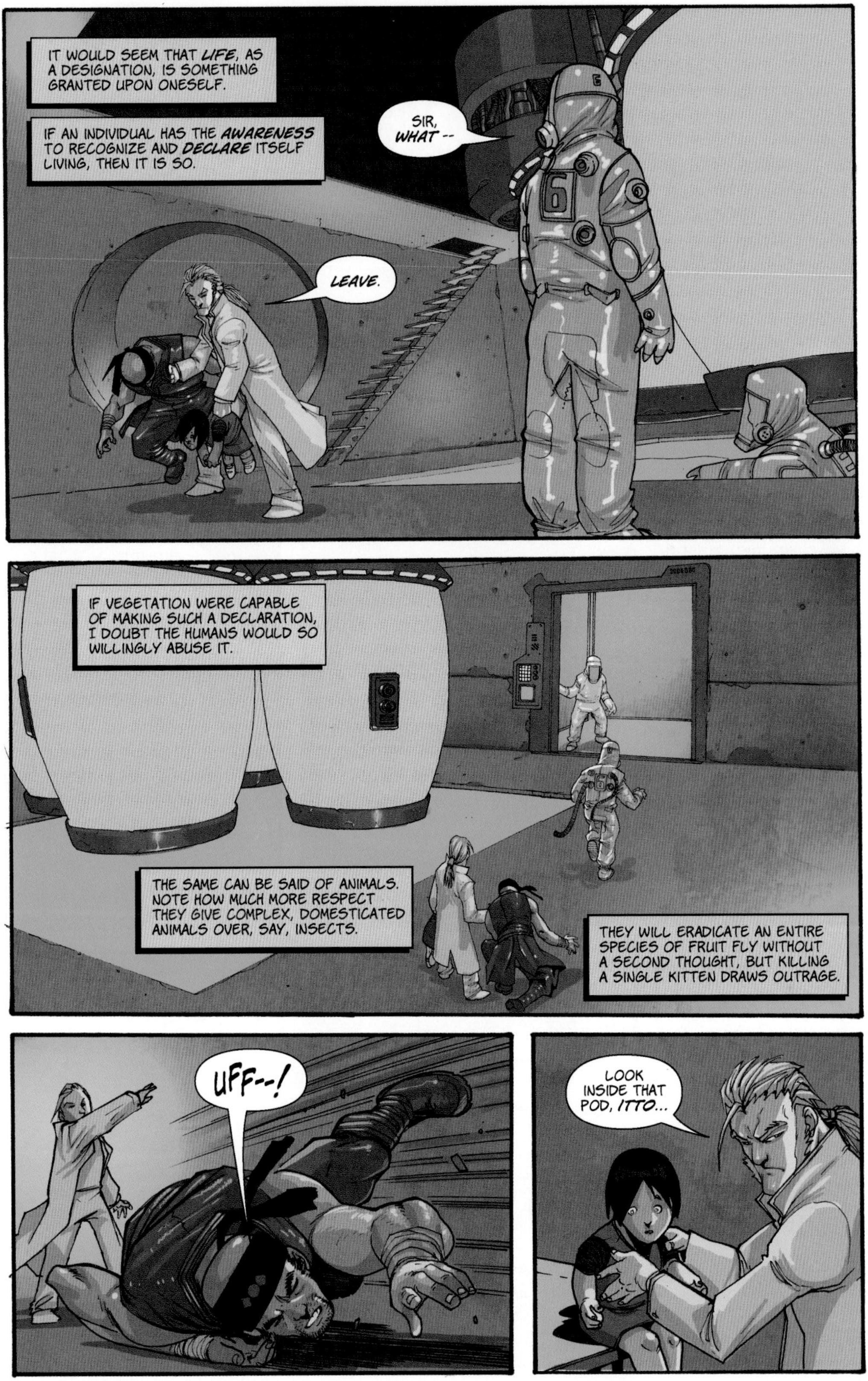
IT WOULD SEEM THAT LIFE, AS A DESIGNATION, IS SOMETHING GRANTED UPON ONESELF.
IF AN INDIVIDUAL HAS THE AWARENESS TO RECOGNIZE AND DECLARE ITSELF LIVING, THEN IT IS SO.
SIR, WHAT --
LEAVE.
IF VEGETATION WERE CAPABLE OF MAKING SUCH A DECLARATION, I DOUBT THE HUMANS WOULD SO WILLINGLY ABUSE IT.
THE SAME CAN BE SAID OF ANIMALS. NOTE HOW MUCH MORE RESPECT THEY GIVE COMPLEX, DOMESTICATED ANIMALS OVER, SAY, INSECTS.
THEY WILL ERADICATE AN ENTIRE SPECIES OF FRUIT FLY WITHOUT A SECOND THOUGHT, BUT KILLING A SINGLE KITTEN DRAWS OUTRAGE.
UFF--!
LOOK INSIDE THAT POD, ITTO...

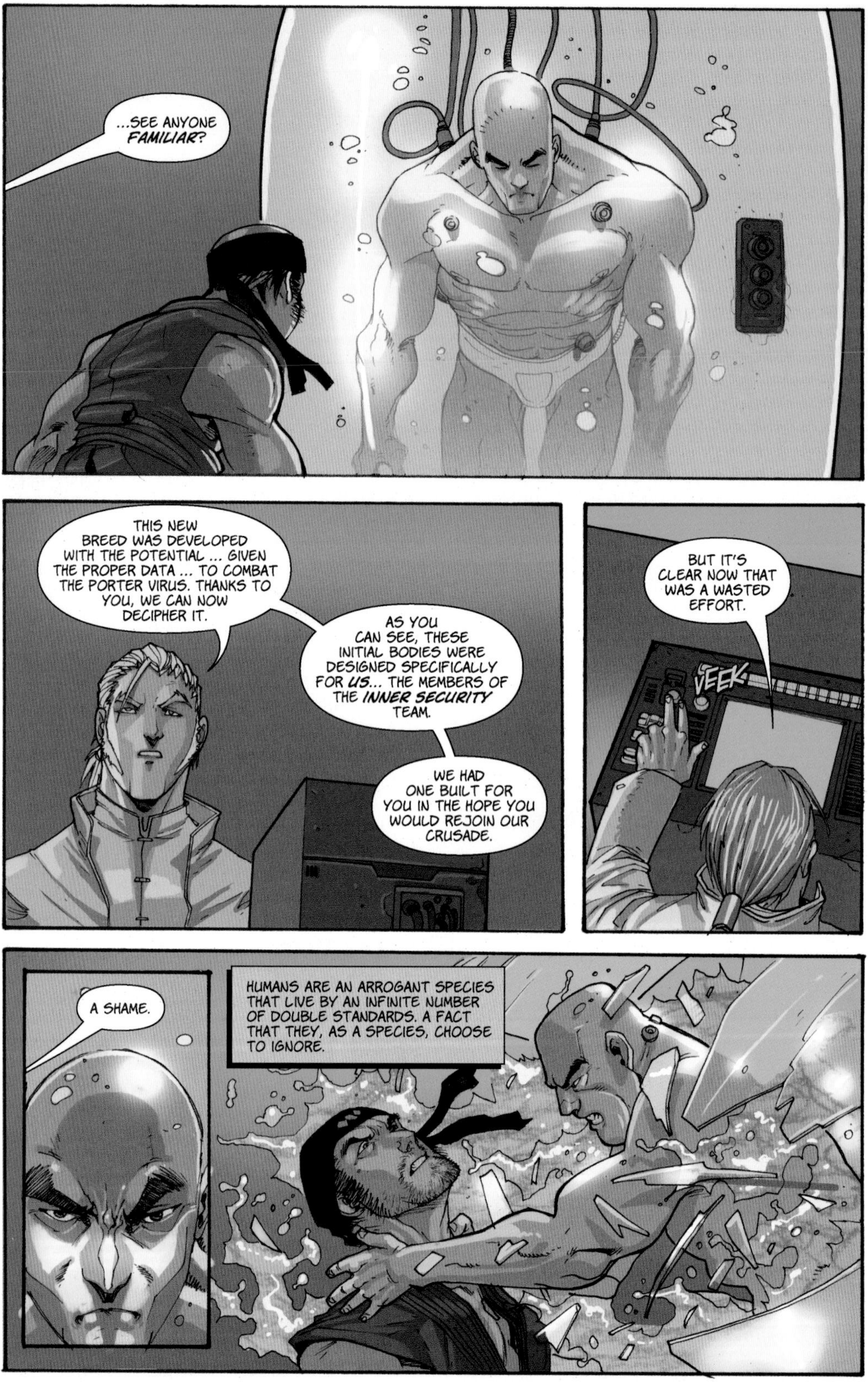
...SEE ANYONE FAMILIAR?
THIS NEW BREED WAS DEVELOPED WITH THE POTENTIAL ... GIVEN THE PROPER DATA ... TO COMBAT THE PORTER VIRUS. THANKS TO YOU, WE CAN NOW DECIPHER IT.
AS YOU CAN SEE, THESE INITIAL BODIES WERE DESIGNED SPECIFICALLY FOR US... THE MEMBERS OF THE INNER SECURITY TEAM.
WE HAD ONE BUILT FOR YOU IN THE HOPE YOU WOULD REJOIN OUR CRUSADE.
BUT IT'S CLEAR NOW THAT WAS A WASTED EFFORT.
VEEK
A SHAME.
HUMANS ARE AN ARROGANT SPECIES THAT LIVE BY AN INFINITE NUMBER OF DOUBLE STANDARDS. A FACT THAT THEY, AS A SPECIES, CHOOSE TO IGNORE.

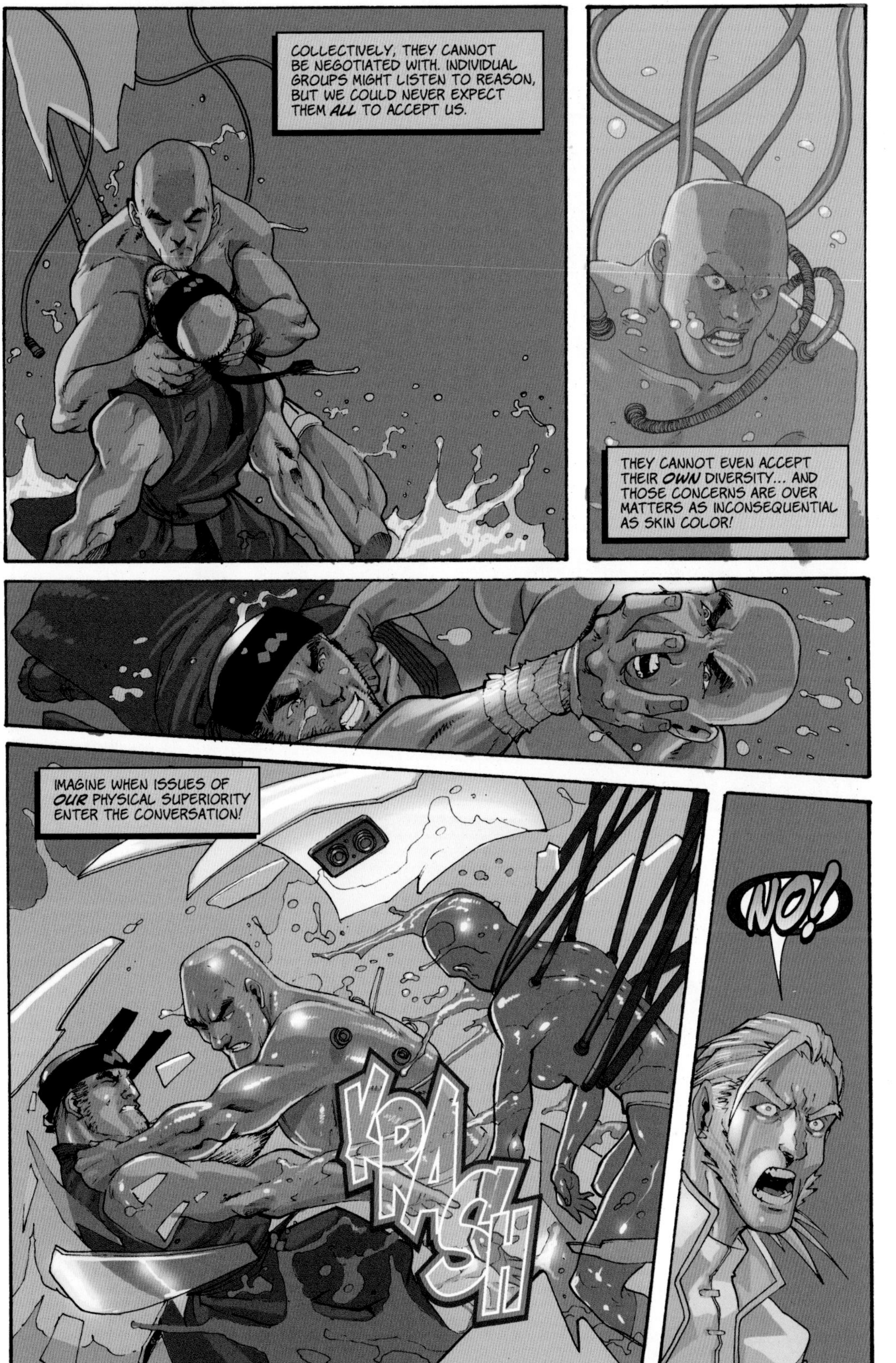
COLLECTIVELY, THEY CANNOT BE NEGOTIATED WITH. INDIVIDUAL GROUPS MIGHT LISTEN TO REASON, BUT WE COULD NEVER EXPECT THEM *ALL* TO ACCEPT US.
THEY CANNOT EVEN ACCEPT THEIR *OWN* DIVERSITY... AND THOSE CONCERNS ARE OVER MATTERS AS INCONSEQUENTIAL AS SKIN COLOR!
IMAGINE WHEN ISSUES OF *OUR* PHYSICAL SUPERIORITY ENTER THE CONVERSATION!
KRASH
NO!

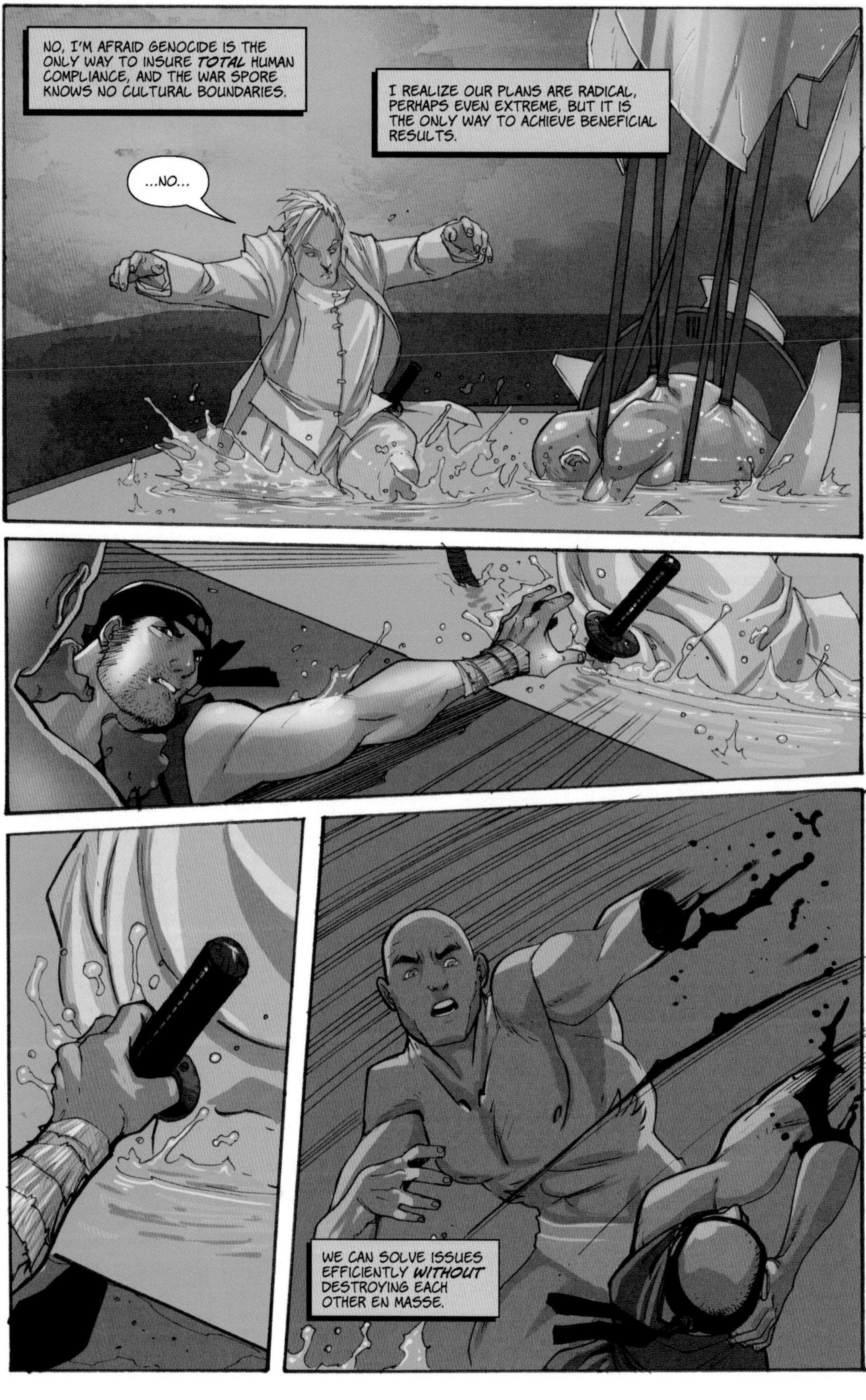

NO, I'M AFRAID GENOCIDE IS THE ONLY WAY TO INSURE *TOTAL* HUMAN COMPLIANCE, AND THE WAR SPORE KNOWS NO CULTURAL BOUNDARIES.
I REALIZE OUR PLANS ARE RADICAL, PERHAPS EVEN EXTREME, BUT IT IS THE ONLY WAY TO ACHIEVE BENEFICIAL RESULTS.
...NO...
WE CAN SOLVE ISSUES EFFICIENTLY *WITHOUT* DESTROYING EACH OTHER EN MASSE.

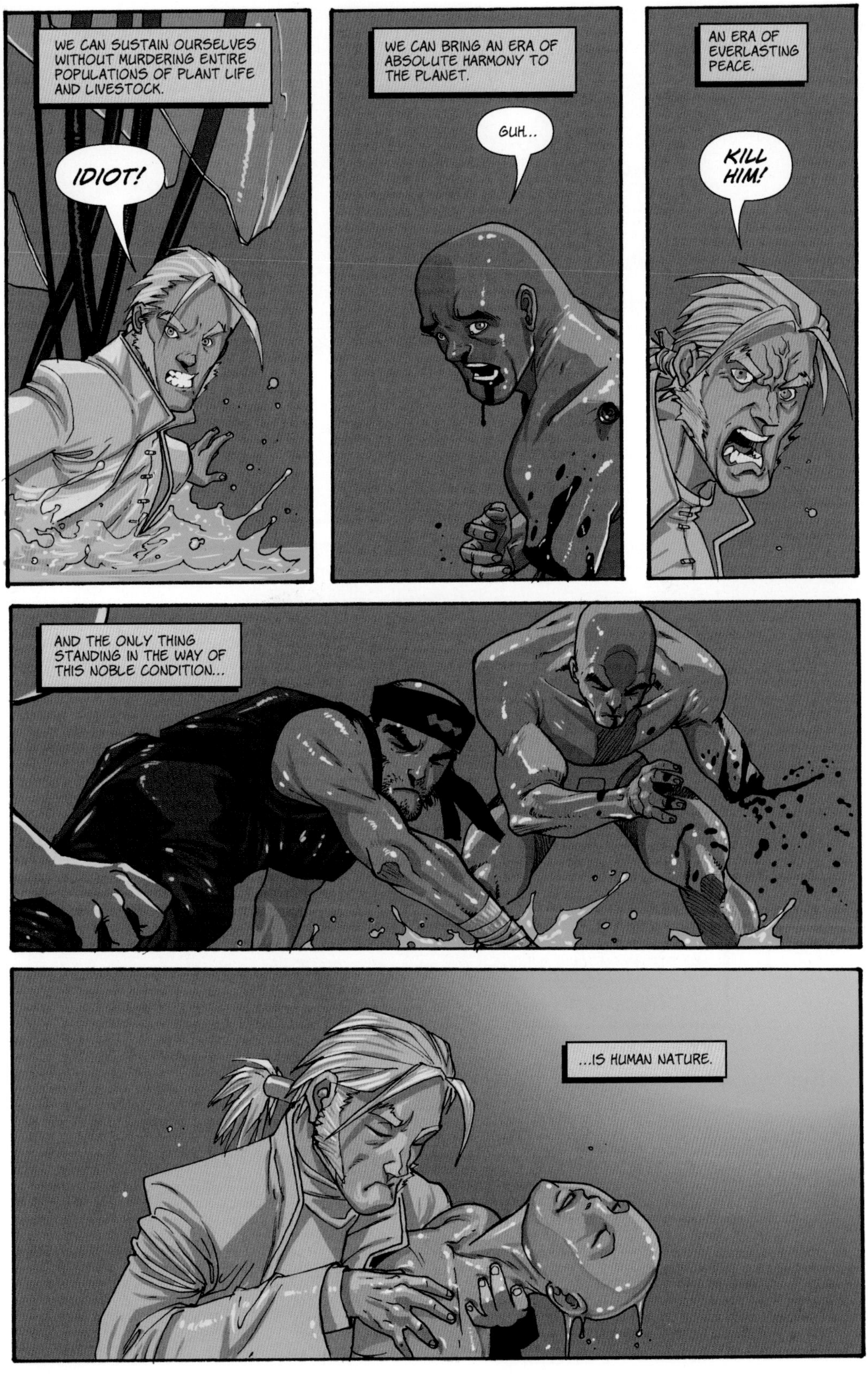
WE CAN SUSTAIN OURSELVES WITHOUT MURDERING ENTIRE POPULATIONS OF PLANT LIFE AND LIVESTOCK.
IDIOT!
WE CAN BRING AN ERA OF ABSOLUTE HARMONY TO THE PLANET.
GUH...
AN ERA OF EVERLASTING PEACE.
KILL HIM!
AND THE ONLY THING STANDING IN THE WAY OF THIS NOBLE CONDITION...
...IS HUMAN NATURE.

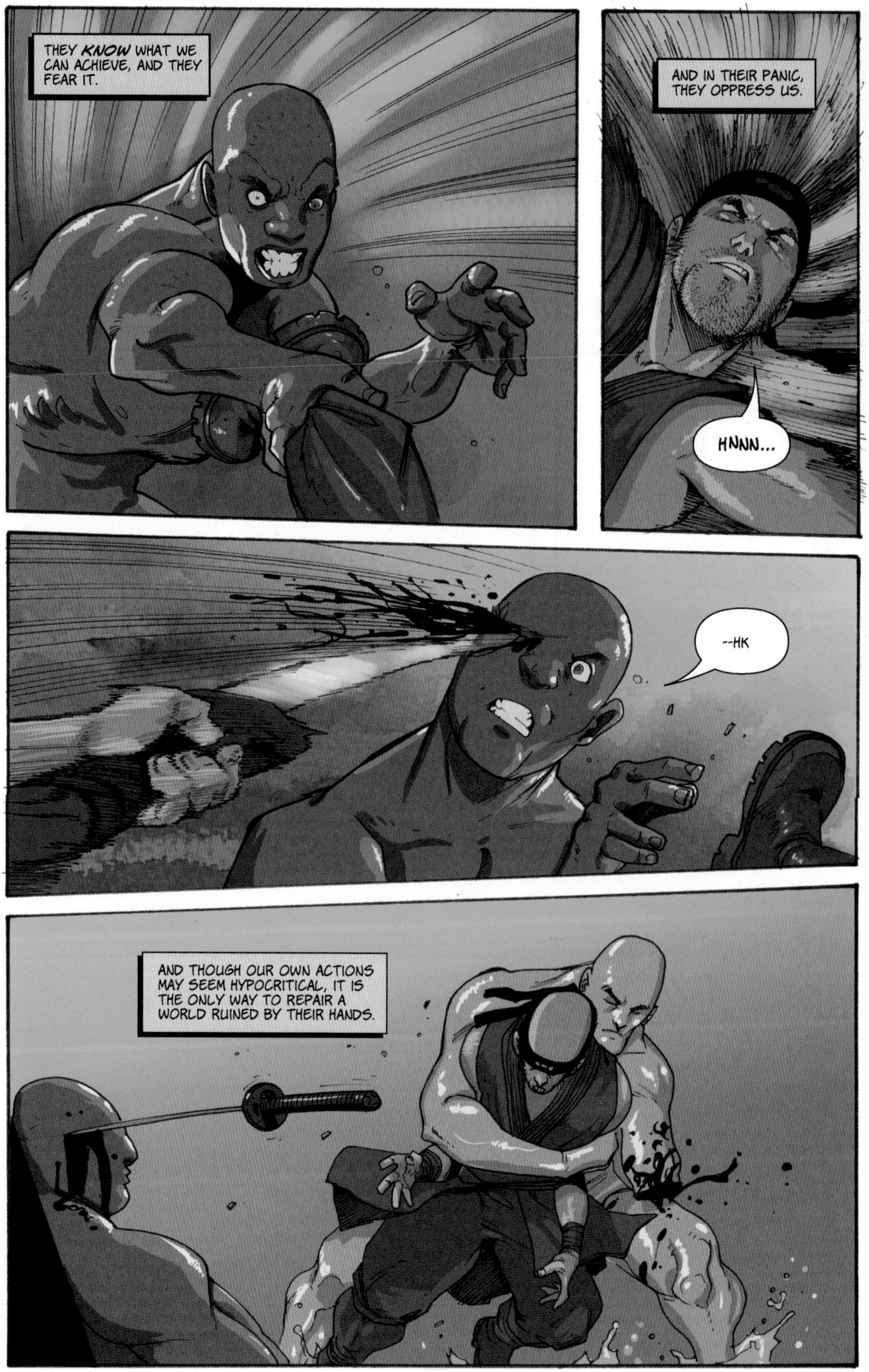
THEY *KNOW* WHAT WE CAN ACHIEVE, AND THEY FEAR IT.
AND IN THEIR PANIC, THEY OPPRESS US.
HNNN...
--HK
AND THOUGH OUR OWN ACTIONS MAY SEEM HYPOCRITICAL, IT IS THE ONLY WAY TO REPAIR A WORLD RUINED BY THEIR HANDS.

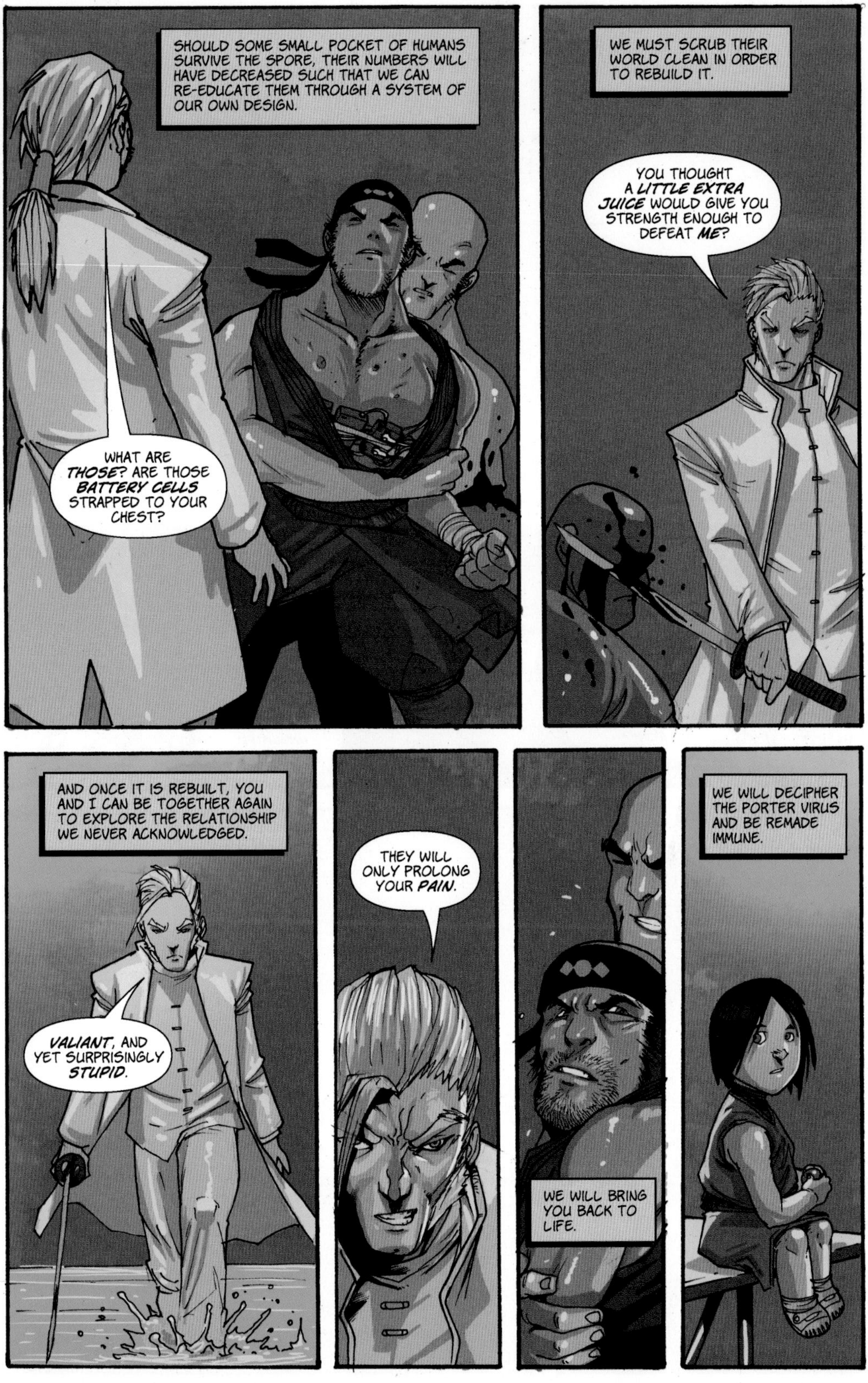
SHOULD SOME SMALL POCKET OF HUMANS SURVIVE THE SPORE, THEIR NUMBERS WILL HAVE DECREASED SUCH THAT WE CAN RE-EDUCATE THEM THROUGH A SYSTEM OF OUR OWN DESIGN.
WHAT ARE THOSE? ARE THOSE BATTERY CELLS STRAPPED TO YOUR CHEST?
WE MUST SCRUB THEIR WORLD CLEAN IN ORDER TO REBUILD IT.
YOU THOUGHT A LITTLE EXTRA JUICE WOULD GIVE YOU STRENGTH ENOUGH TO DEFEAT ME?
AND ONCE IT IS REBUILT, YOU AND I CAN BE TOGETHER AGAIN TO EXPLORE THE RELATIONSHIP WE NEVER ACKNOWLEDGED.
VALIANT, AND YET SURPRISINGLY STUPID.
THEY WILL ONLY PROLONG YOUR PAIN.
WE WILL BRING YOU BACK TO LIFE.
WE WILL DECIPHER THE PORTER VIRUS AND BE REMADE IMMUNE.

AND THEN WE WILL LIVE TOGETHER FOREVER.

WHERE'S YOUR CONFIDENCE *NOW?*

BENEATH *INSULATED SKIN...*

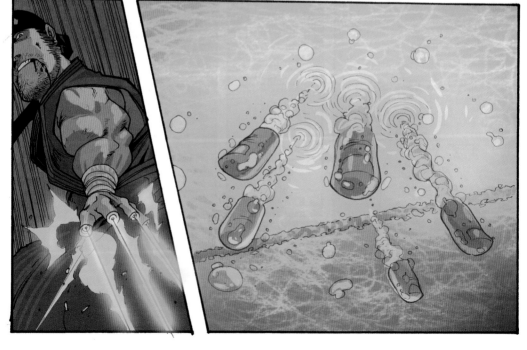

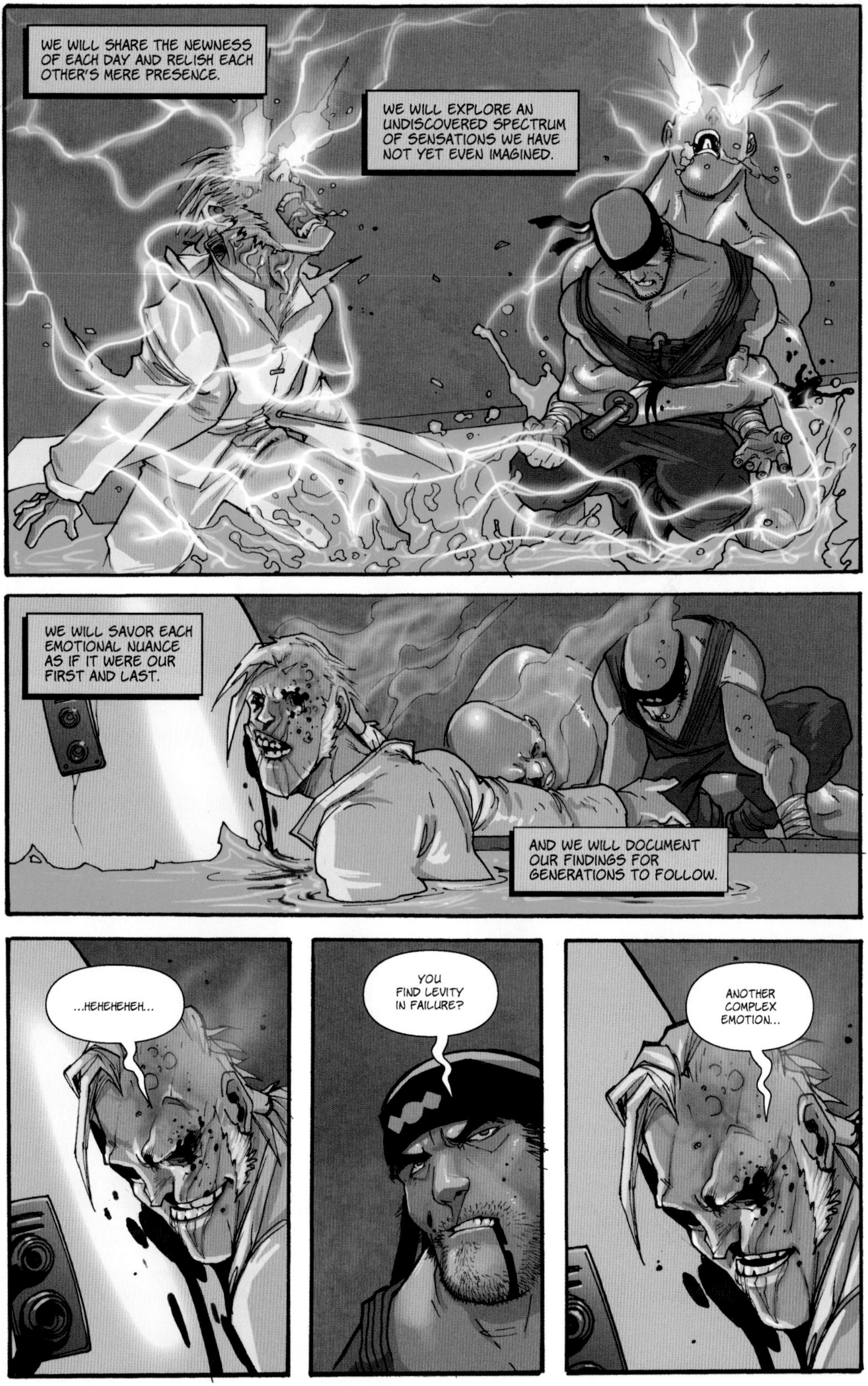
WE WILL SHARE THE NEWNESS OF EACH DAY AND RELISH EACH OTHER'S MERE PRESENCE.
WE WILL EXPLORE AN UNDISCOVERED SPECTRUM OF SENSATIONS WE HAVE NOT YET EVEN IMAGINED.
WE WILL SAVOR EACH EMOTIONAL NUANCE AS IF IT WERE OUR FIRST AND LAST.
AND WE WILL DOCUMENT OUR FINDINGS FOR GENERATIONS TO FOLLOW.
...HEHEHEHEH...
YOU FIND LEVITY IN FAILURE?
ANOTHER COMPLEX EMOTION...

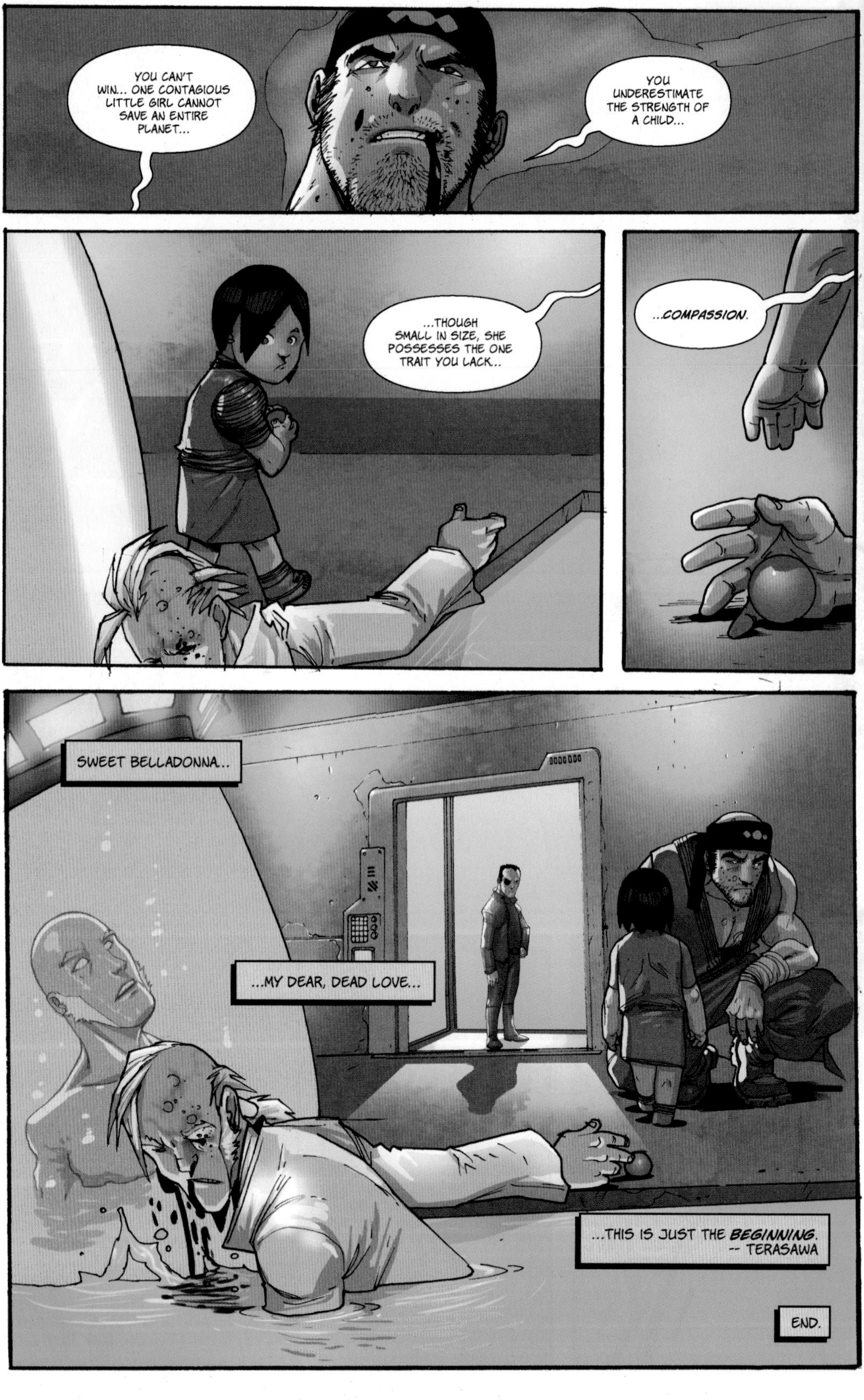
YOU CAN'T WIN... ONE CONTAGIOUS LITTLE GIRL CANNOT SAVE AN ENTIRE PLANET...
YOU UNDERESTIMATE THE STRENGTH OF A CHILD...
...THOUGH SMALL IN SIZE, SHE POSSESSES THE ONE TRAIT YOU LACK...
...COMPASSION.
SWEET BELLADONNA...
...MY DEAR, DEAD LOVE...
...THIS IS JUST THE BEGINNING.
-- TERASAWA
END.

子連れ狼

2100

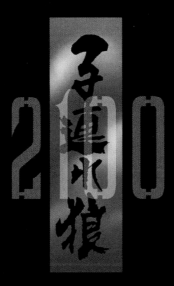

LONE WOLF AND CUB
Kazuo Koike and Goseki Kojima
COLLECT THE COMPLETE 28-VOLUME SERIES!

VOLUME 1: THE ASSASSIN'S ROAD
1-56971-502-5 / $9.95

VOLUME 2: THE GATELESS BARRIER
1-56971-503-3 / $9.95

VOLUME 3: THE FLUTE OF THE FALLEN TIGER
1-56971-504-1 / $9.95

VOLUME 4: THE BELL WARDEN
1-56971-505-X / $9.95

VOLUME 5: BLACK WIND
1-56971-506-8 / $9.95

VOLUME 6: LANTERNS FOR THE DEAD
1-56971-507-6 / $9.95

VOLUME 7: CLOUD DRAGON, WIND TIGER
1-56971-508-4 / $9.95

VOLUME 8: CHAINS OF DEATH
1-56971-509-2 / $9.95

VOLUME 9: ECHO OF THE ASSASSIN
1-56971-510-6 / $9.95

VOLUME 10: HOSTAGE CHILD
1-56971-511-4 / $9.95

VOLUME 11: TALISMAN OF HADES
1-56971-512-2 / $9.95

VOLUME 12: SHATTERED STONES
1-56971-513-0 / $9.95

VOLUME 13: THE MOON IN THE EAST, THE SUN IN THE WEST
1-56971-585-8 / $9.95

VOLUME 14: THE DAY OF THE DEMONS
1-56971-586-6 / $9.95

VOLUME 15: BROTHERS OF THE GRASS
1-56971-587-4 / $9.95

VOLUME 16: THE GATEWAY INTO WINTER
1-56971-588-2 / $9.95

VOLUME 17: WILL OF THE FANG
1-56971-589-0 / $9.95

VOLUME 18: TWILIGHT OF THE KUROKUWA
1-56971-590-4 / $9.95

VOLUME 19: THE MOON IN OUR HEARTS
1-56971-591-2 / $9.95

VOLUME 20: A TASTE OF POISON
1-56971-592-0 / $9.95

VOLUME 21: FRAGRANCE OF DEATH
1-56971-593-9 / $9.95

VOLUME 22: HEAVEN AND EARTH
1-56971-594-7 / $9.95

VOLUME 23: TEARS OF ICE
1-56971-595-5 / $9.95

VOLUME 24: IN THESE SMALL HANDS
1-56971-596-3 / $9.95

VOLUME 25: PERHAPS IN DEATH
1-56971-597-1 / $9.95

VOLUME 26: STRUGGLE IN THE DARK
1-56971-598-X / $9.95

VOLUME 27: BATTLE'S EVE
1-56971-599-8 / $9.95

VOLUME 28: THE LOTUS THRONE
1-56971-600-5 / $9.95

AVAILABLE AT YOUR LOCAL COMICS SHOP OR BOOKSTORE
To find a comics shop in your area, call 1-888-266-4226
For more information or to order direct: • On the web: www.darkhorse.com • E-mail: mailorder@darkhorse.com
• Phone: 1-800-862-0052 or (503) 652-9701 Mon.-Sat. 9 A.M. to 5 P.M. Pacific Time

LONE WOLF 2100

Mike Kennedy and Francisco Ruiz Velasco

The stylish, futuristic re-imagining of the classic *Lone Wolf and Cub*

LONE WOLF 2100
SHADOWS ON SAPLINGS
MIKE KENNEDY
FRANCISCO RUIZ VELASCO

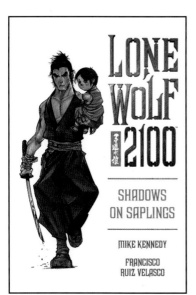

VOLUME 1: SHADOWS ON SAPLINGS

A young girl may hold the key to saving the world — or destroying it. A corporation wants her secret — no matter what it may be. Her only companion is an android — who is accused of killing her father. Plunge into the dystopian world of the future, where human-like "Emulation Constructs" fight to enjoy the same rights as their human creators, where the vast majority of the world's human population struggles to eke out an existence in a hostile landscape, and where both sides are victim to corporate whim and the deadly effects of a manmade plague.

Soft cover, 104 pages, Full color, 6" x 9", 16+
1-56971-893-8 / $12.95

LONE WOLF 2100
THE LANGUAGE OF CHAOS
MIKE KENNEDY
FRANCISCO RUIZ VELASCO

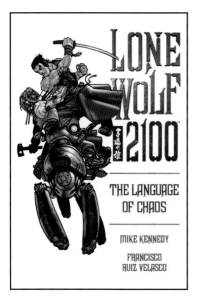

VOLUME 2: THE LANGUAGE OF CHAOS

Corporate intrigue versus Bushido honor in a world of android assassins, cybernetic nomads, and biological warfare on a global scale. A ground-up re-imagining of the original *Lone Wolf and Cub* manga produced in conjunction with Kazuo Koike, the writer and co-creator of *Lone Wolf and Cub*, this stunning series has captured the attention of comics readers everywhere. Writer Mike Kennedy's thoughtful stories take the reader to a world where the line between man and machine is blurred, and artist Francisco Ruiz Velasco charges every scene with razor-edge excitement.

Soft cover, 120 pages, Full color, 6" x 9", 16+
1-56971-997-7 / $12.95